Le vetrine del sapere. 10

EGYPT AND THE PHARAOHS

From Conservation to Enjoyment

Pharaonic Egypt in the Archives and Libraries
of the Università degli Studi di Milano

Editor
Patrizia Piacentini

Texts by
Laura Marucchi, Fernando Mazzocca, Antonello Negri,
Christian Orsenigo, Patrizia Piacentini, Marta Sironi

Università degli Studi di Milano

SKIRA

Project Management
Studio Redazionale Sigma Rho, Milano

Translators
Helen Downes
Marco Biaggi
Patrizia Piacentini

Digitization of documents
Marco Biaggi
Laura Marucchi

Photos
Carlo Vannini, pp. 27, 36-37, 42-43, 132, 135, 137, 139-144
Galleria Nazionale d'Arte Moderna e Contemporanea, Roma,
su gentile concessione del Ministero per i Beni e le Attività
Culturali, p. 78
Pinacoteca di Brera, Milano, Electa Photoservice p. 79
Birmingham Museums and Art Gallery, Birmingham p. 81
Rijksmuseum, Amsterdam p. 83
Musea Brugge©Lukas-Art in Flanders vzw, Royal Museum
of Fine Arts, Antwerp pp. 85, 86
Fototeca Alinari, Firenze p. 88
Istituzione Galleria d'Arte Moderna di Bologna,
Collezioni Storiche, Bologna pp. 90, 91
Museo Richard-Ginori della Manifattura di Doccia,
Sesto Fiorentino p. 97
Cooper-Hewitt Museum, New York City,
Archivio Scala, Firenze p. 107
Biblioteca dell'Archiginnasio, Bologna,
Fornasini Microfilm Service p. 116
Museo Internazionale e Biblioteca della Musica, Bologna,
Fornasini Microfilm Service pp. 117, 118

Reproduction
Graphic srl, Milano

First published in 2011 by
Skira Editore S.p.A.
Palazzo Casati Stampa
via Torino 61
20123 Milano
Italy
www.skira.net

Printed and bound in Italy. First edition

ISBN 978-88-572-1274-6

Distributed in USA, Canada, Central & South America
by Rizzoli International Publications, Inc.,
300 Park Avenue South, New York, NY 10010, USA.
Distributed elsewhere in the world by
Thames and Hudson Ltd., 181A High Holborn,
London WC1V 7QX, United Kingdom.

The present volume has been printed with the financial contribution of Goppion S.p.A.
and Associazione *Per-megiat* onlus per la tutela e la valorizzazione
delle Biblioteche sull'Antico Egitto

The Università degli Studi di Milano takes the opportunity to warmly thank:

Fondazione CARIPLO
Associazione *Per-megiat* onlus per la tutela e la valorizzazione
delle Biblioteche sull'antico Egitto
Maria Petra Bevilacqua Ariosti
Clara Botti
Paola Botti
Eugenio Busmanti
Alessandro Goppion
Solange Lacau
Marie-Jeanne Lacau-Bodolec
Gabriella Robiglio
Elmar W. Seibel
William Kelly Simpson

Gail S. Davidson, *Cooper-Hewitt Museum, New York City*
Allison Derrett, *Royal Archives, Windsor Castle, Windsor*
Eva Fuchs, *Collezioni MAMbo / Museo d'Arte Moderna di Bologna, Bologna*
Roberto Giovanelli, *Museo Richard-Ginori della Manifattura di Doccia, Sesto Fiorentino*
Gianfranco Maraniello, *Collezioni MAMbo / Museo d'Arte Moderna di Bologna, Bologna*
Jonathan Marsden, *Royal Collection, London*
Kathryn Jones, *Royal Collection, London*
Oliva Rucellai, *Museo Richard-Ginori della Manifattura di Doccia, Sesto Fiorentino*
Sabrina Samorì, *Collezioni MAMbo / Museo d'Arte Moderna di Bologna, Bologna*

Publishing Managers
Graziella Buccellati, Benedetta Manetti

English Copy-Editor
Caroline Brooke Johnson

Contents

IX   *Introduction*
Patrizia Piacentini

The Dawn of Museums and Photography in Egypt

5   I. *The Preservation of Antiquities*
Creation of Museums in Egypt during the Nineteenth Century
Patrizia Piacentini

5   *The Beginning of Antiquities Preservation: 1820-1835*
6   *The First Collection: from Ezbekieh to the Citadel*
6   *Auguste Mariette, the "Temple of Armachis"*
and the Museum of Bulaq
14   *Gaston Maspero and Victor Loret in Egypt*
17   *The Graeco-Roman Museum in Alexandria*
and the Provincial Museums
20   *The Giza Museum*
23   *The International Competition for a New Egyptian Museum*
26   *The Construction and Opening of the New Museum*
26   *The Museum's Sale Room*
28   *From the First Renovation of the Museum to New Projects*

45   II. *Photographers in Egypt 1850-1950*
Laura Marucchi, Patrizia Piacentini

Egypt in Modern Culture

75   III. *Aspects of Ancient Egypt*
in Nineteenth Century Painting
Fernando Mazzocca

87   IV. *Walls and Dishes*
Gaetano Lodi, an Italian Painter for the Khedive Ismail Pasha
Patrizia Piacentini

119   V. *Egypt as an Allegory of the Modern Age*
Political Satire, Illustration, and Imagérie populaire
Antonello Negri, Marta Sironi

131   VI. *Egypt in the Box*
Pharaonic Inspiration in Everyday Life
Patrizia Piacentini

Appendices

145   *Chronological Table*

149   *Egyptological Archives and Library*
      of the Università degli Studi di Milano.
      Bibliography (1999-2011)
      Christian Orsenigo

155   *Bibliography*

159   *Index of Names and Places*
      Sara Mastropaolo, Christian Orsenigo

Introduction

Patrizia Piacentini

The Egyptological Archives and Library of the University of Milan have been created over the last decade, beginning in 1999. Their history and contents have been presented in detail in the first of the present volumes, *Egypt and the Pharaohs. From the Sand to the Library*, as well as in other publications, exhibitions, conferences, and lectures. In this second volume, we deal with the conservation of the Egyptian antiquities, their reproduction with photography and painting and their utilization as source of inspiration in art, illustration, advertisement, style, and fashion. Most of the scientific and iconographic material used for each chapter of the present book comes either from the Egyptological Archives or the APICE collections of the University of Milan, but we had the chance to use also other documents, often unpublished, kept in private collections or in Museums.

In the first chapter, I describe how during the nineteenth century the first steps were taken to protect Egypt's archaeological heritage, how the first museums were founded, among them the Egyptian Museum in Cairo and the Graeco-Roman Museum in Alexandria. Many aspects of the birth and early development of this last collection are illustrated in a series of letters written by its founder and first curator, Giuseppe Botti "the First", and deposited in the Egyptological Archives of the University of Milan by the heirs of this great scholar. Another important source of information is provided by the documents preserved in the Loret and Lacau collections of the University. The history of the Cairo Egyptian Museum, in its successive locations in Bulaq, Giza, and central Cairo – today Tahrir Square – has been reconstructed from a new perspective thanks to the large number of documents preserved in the Milanese Archives. This was featured in *The History of the Egyptian Museum*, an exhibition organized by the Chair of Egyptology of the University of Milan and the Direction of the Egyptian Museum in Cairo, where it was held from October 19, 2008 to January 31, 2009. The exhibition was viewed not only by the many international visitors of the Museum – among them the President of the Italian Republic, Giorgio Napolitano – but also, and perhaps even more, by the Egyptian public, who were able to discover previously unknown episodes relating to the creation of one of the most important institutions in their own country and its development during the 150 years following its foundation.

Through images of rare beauty, Laura Marucchi and myself recount the history of the early photographers in Egypt and present the first aerial photographs taken there by Kofler, a little-known photographer who is currently the focus of intensive research. The authors also describe photographic experimentation and the development of photographic techniques applied to archaeology.

One section of the volume deals with Egypt's "fortunes" in modern culture. Starting with painting, the essay by Fernando Mazzocca outlines the aspects of ancient Egypt most commonly featured in nineteenth-century paintings, concentrating in particular on those by artists from Lombardy.

In the subsequent chapter the works of Egyptian inspiration by

Facing page:
The Università degli Studi di Milano, detail of the Porticoes.
University of Milan Archives

IX

the Italian painter and ornamentist, Gaetano Lodi, are illustrated and critically analyzed. After working on the decoration of the foyer of the Paris Opera House and the Galleria Vittorio Emanuele in Milan, Lodi left for Egypt in 1872, where one of his assignments was to decorate the palace of the Viceroy Ismail Pasha at Giza. In the final decade of the nineteenth century, the palace became for a while the seat of the Egyptian Museum in Cairo. While in Egypt, Lodi also made preliminary sketches for a porcelain service in "Egyptian style," commissioned by the Viceroy and produced by the Ginori factory. Thanks to an exceptional series of watercolors submitted for study to the Chair of Egyptology of the University of Milan, and by comparing these with some of the pieces preserved in the Richard-Ginori Museum of the Doccia factory at Sesto Fiorentino, it has been possible to prove that Lodi was responsible for the refined design of the service. Lodi also decorated in Egyptian style a room in a palace in Bologna, which is a fine example of the Egyptian Revival in Italy in the second half of the nineteenth century.

The image of Egypt, as it was formed and consolidated, starting from the expedition of Napoleon Bonaparte in 1798-99 and through subsequent waves of Egyptomania, is also reflected in art, books, and twentieth-century periodicals kept in the Archives of the APICE Center of the University of Milan. Antonello Negri's and Marta Sironi's contribution is devoted to this subject.

The Egyptological Archives contain also a remarkable collection of objects and watercolors from the nineteenth and twentieth centuries, inspired by ancient Egypt, among which a series of more than eight hundred cigarette-boxes or labels in Egyptian style. They exemplify the cultural phenomenon known as Egyptomania, an area of research that the Chair of Egyptology of the University of Milan has been specifically engaged in for many years. A lavishly illustrated chapter is written by myself on this subject.

I am greatly indebted to the authors who have contributed to this volume, transforming relevant information from the University's Archives and enriching it with their own scholarship.

I express my profound gratitude to the donors who have provided the Archives with their own collections or with documents and books found on the antiquarian market, as well as to the CARIPLO Foundation, for its financial support in acquiring part of the Egyptological Library and for the conservation and restoration of archival documents.

Special thanks go to to all the friends and colleagues who, in differing ways, have graciously helped me since my arrival in the University in 1993.

I also warmly thank Graziella Buccellati and Benedetta Manetti for editing, project managing and creatively contributing to this book.

Our most profound thanks have to be reserved for Professor Enrico Decleva, Rector of the Università degli Studi di Milano, for his enthusiastic encouragement of the original idea to build an Egyptological Library at our University, and its subsequent expansion to include archival collections as well, and for his advice and support over the years.

Facing page:
Scene from the Tomb of Pashed at Deir el-Medina (TT 3). Watercolor.
Eg. Arch. & Lib., Loret Collection

Following page:
C. & G. Zangaki, *Dahabiya* on the Nile.
Eg. Arch. & Lib.

N° 431 Dahabieh et pont de Kasr-el-Nil

The Dawn of Museums and Photography in Egypt

The Preservation of Antiquities
Creation of Museums in Egypt during the Nineteenth Century

Patrizia Piacentini

I. *The Preservation of Antiquities*

Creation of Museums in Egypt during the Nineteenth Century

Patrizia Piacentini

The Beginning of Antiquities Preservation: 1820-1835

From 1820, the Khedive of Egypt Mohamed Ali issued decrees to regulate destructive excavations and the uncontrolled exportation of antiquities, including the colossal ones.

The first decree, dated 1820, was intended to restrain the work of Captain Giovanni Battista Caviglia; a further decree, dated May 1826, concerned the prohibition of removing ancient stones that had been reused in the construction of mosques:

Nous ne sommes pas d'accord pour donner aux Anglais la pierre ancienne se trouvant au seuil de la mosquée située à Bab el-Nasr [...] il nous est impossible de leur permettre pareille chose ; [...] si nous leur accordons volontiers toutes les pierres qui se trouvent en divers lieux, il ne convient pas de leur accorder celles qui font partie des mosquées.
(D. ABOU-GHAZI, "The First Egyptian Museum", in *ASAE* 67, 1988, pp. 1-2)

In April 1832, the Khedive regulated John Gardner Wilkinson's activities, and the following year the excavations in the provinces:

Il est demandé à Hussein Heidar Bey de fouiller dans la province de la Galioubieh, près du lieu où l'on trouva la pierre antique qui fut envoyée à Son Altesse [...] ; de désigner un Moawen pour surveiller les fouilles, car il est possible d'y trouver d'autres antiquités, qui ne doivent pas passer des mains des ouvriers à celles des Européens.
(A. KHATER, *Le régime juridique des fouilles et des antiquités en Égypte*, Le Caire 1960, p. 33)

This growing awareness of the importance of preserving ancient monuments was crowned in August 1835 when, in order to block the exportation of the collection assembled by Mimaut, the consul of France, the Khedive issued a decree that resulted in the creation of an Antiquities Service and an Egyptian museum in Cairo. This happened despite there still being confusion between the public and the personal properties of the Khedive. Moreover, the museum seemed to be more an antiquities deposit than a visitor attraction.

In the first thirty years of the nineteenth century, Egyptian monuments were both extensively pillaged by Europeans and subjected to the greed or neglect of the locals, who did not hesitate to destroy them just to get construction stones or to take lime.

Even though Champollion had left Egypt with a great quantity of important objects destined for the Louvre, in November 1829 he himself addressed a report to Mohamed Ali, upon his request, on the state of ancient monuments in the country and on the need of creating an institution to preserve antiquities.

Facing page:
Napoleon's headquarters at Ezbekieh.
In one of these buildings was housed the first collection of Egyptian antiquities,
in J. DE METZ, G. LEGRAIN, *Au Pays de Napoléon. L'Égypte*, Grenoble 1913, p. 102.
Eg. Arch. & Lib., Varille Collection

The Ezbekieh Gardens in Cairo.
Photograph by J.P. Sebah.
Eg. Arch. & Lib., Private Collection (long term deposit)

The First Collection: from Ezbekieh to the Citadel

According to the 1835 decree, the objects found in Egypt were to be sent to Sheikh Rifaa el-Tahtawi, a famous Egyptian intellectual of the time, and put under the direction of Yusuf Diya Effendi, who was also responsible for inspecting archaeological sites periodically. This growing collection was housed in some unused rooms of the School of Languages at Ezbekieh, in the center of Cairo, and more precisely in the southern wing of the palace of the defterdar, Elfy Bey. At the time, the Armenian engineer Yusuf Bey Hekekian was in charge of renovating the palace, which, together with the adjacent buildings, had been the headquarters of Napoleon and his officials during the expedition in Egypt of 1798-99.

After their destruction, the famous Shepheard's Hotel was build in the same place, but this building was also destroyed by a fire during the turmoil and riots of 1952.

Nevertheless, only a few of the objects reached this kind of newly instituted museum, because they were stolen or lost during transportation or on arrival. In 1848-49, Linant de Bellefonds was put in charge of drawing up an inventory of the collected objects, with the view to move them, first to a school in the Sayedah Zeinab area, and then, because of the smallness of the location, to a warehouse at the Engineers School at Bulaq. The transfer was ordered in October 1849 by Abbas Pasha. At this time, the occidental intellectual milieu also began to deplore the systematic destruction or despoiling of Egyptian monuments, as confirmed by an appeal submitted by Lord Algernon Percy in 1836; by the report on the disastrous situation relating to Egypt's antiquities sent to the Khedive by Lord Bowring; or by the 1841's memorandum by George Robins Gliddon, the American consul in Cairo. These warnings had no effect, and when the objects of the first museum at Ezbekieh were transferred to the building of the Ministry of Education at the Citadel in around 1851, there were so few artefacts that they could all be put in a single hall, also used by the Ministry's employees to store their coats and food. Between 1852 and 1854, a few stele found by Mariette in the Serapeum were deposited there, but in 1855 most of the objects were offered to Archduke Maximilian of Austria during his visit in Egypt as official state gift. These are now included in the Egyptian collection of the Kunsthistorisches Museum in Vienna.

Auguste Mariette, the "Temple of Armachis" and the Museum of Bulaq

Auguste Mariette, who was successfully excavating in Egypt and who still believed in the need to stop the progressive dispersal of Egyptian heritage, was able, with the help of Ferdinand de Lesseps, to convince the new Khedive Said Pasha of the need for an effective Antiquities Service. This institution had to decide, among other things, which objects should stay in Egypt and which ones could be offered or sold abroad. On June 1, 1858 Mariette was appointed as the Director of the Service. The first stages of the new institution were narrated by the French scholar to the friend and colleague Heinrich Brugsch in a famous letter, dated April 10, 1859, preserved in the Egyptological Archives of the University of Milan:

J'ai pour fonctions en Égypte de veiller à ce qu'on ne détruise pas les monuments antiques, et en même temps je crée un Musée pour le Vice-Roi. Un égyptologue ne peut pas avoir de devoirs plus agréables à remplir […].

Caire près du Mokhatam. 44.

At first, Mariette thought of a possible location for the museum at Giza, around the "bizarre édifice situé près du Sphinx," as he used to call the Valley Temple of Chephren that he discovered in 1854:

Quant au Musée je crois fort qu'il se fera aux pyramides mêmes, en utilisant le temple d'Armachis trouvé par moi autrefois. C'est un assez bon emplacement, qui a l'avantage énorme d'être un peu loin des yeux des Turcs lesquels s'offensent un peu à l'idée trop européenne du Vice-Roi de fonder un Musée. Je vais le faire déblayer complètement après le Ramadan et j'espère en faire quelque chose.

The next idea was to build a museum on the Gezireh island, but this was soon abandoned. In the end, the decision was taken to house the collection in the garden and in four rooms of an abandoned building of the Nile Navigation Company in Bulaq harbour. The building was renovated and decorated by Mariette himself in Egyptian style, with the help of his loyal collaborators Bonnefoy and Floris, as Maspero tells:

Choisissant quatre chambres mieux closes que les autres, il les transforma en salle d'exposition pour les monuments les plus beaux et les plus curieux. Un Corse à tout faire du nom de Floris lui improvisa des piédestaux et des vitrines, tandis que lui-même, se souvenant d'avoir été maître de dessin dans sa jeunesse, il peignait sur les murs une décoration sobre et fine.
(G. MASPERO, in *Revue d'Égypte et d'Orient* 7/4, 1906, p. 138)

Mariette probably finished setting-up the museum on October 18, 1863. The date of the opening is not clear: according to Maspero it took place on October 18, whereas from the memories of Félicien de Saulcy it can be deduced that the museum was probably opened after October 23. De Saulcy, friend and supporter of Mariette, stopped in Egypt on his way to the Holy Land in October 1863. On October 19, he visited the new museum, and on the same day he went to pay homage to the Khedive and to tell him, among other things, that Mariette had finished setting-up the museum just the evening before, as he wrote in his work:

À six heures et demie, ce brave ami [*i.e.* Mariette] était à l'hôtel, et nous montions en voiture pour nous rendre à Boulaq, où il a établi son musée. Ce sont les bâtiments délabrés du transit, qui lui ont été livrés par le vice-roi feu Saïd-Pacha, pour y réunir les merveilles inappréciables qu'il lui a été donné de recueillir. Toutes proviennent des fouilles entreprises par lui pour le compte de l'État égyptien. Mariette, en effet, avait facilement fait comprendre au souverain qu'il était déplorable que tous les musées de l'Europe se fussent enrichis aux dépens de l'Égypte ; qu'il était temps de doter son pays d'une fondation digne d'un prince véritablement éclairé, que semblable création d'ailleurs ne manquerait pas de jeter une gloire incontestable sur son règne, en attirant au Caire les égyptologues, dont le nombre allait toujours croissant en Europe, et pour lesquels l'étude d'un pareil trésor ne pouvait manquer de devenir un motif impérieux de visiter eux mêmes la terre des Pharaons. Cette idée toute simple et toute naturelle frappa l'esprit du souverain ; la formation d'un musée égyptien au Caire fut immédiatement décrétée, et les moyens les plus efficaces pour atteindre le but désiré furent mis à la disposition de Mariette. On lui confia l'inspection et la garde de tous les monuments encore existants, avec mission de les déblayer et d'entreprendre où bon lui semblerait les fouilles qui devaient fournir les éléments du futur musée ; le commerce interlope des antiquités fut absolument interdit du même coup, et la destruction pour ainsi dire systématique des monuments fut arrêtée. Espérons qu'elle ne reprendra plus sa désastreuse allure. Il n'y a pas sous le soleil de climat plus conservateur que celui de l'Égypte ; il suffira donc de vouloir désormais, pour que plus rien ne disparaisse de l'inventaire des monuments illustres que quarante siècles de l'histoire humaine ont répandus sur cette terre privilégiée.

Statue of Queen Neferet, wife of Senuseret II, from A. Mariette's excavations at Tanis in 1863. Garden of the Bulaq Museum (Cairo CG 382). Photograph. Eg. Arch. & Lib.

Facing page:
One room of the Bulaq Museum, in A. MARIETTE, *Album du Musée de Boulaq*, Le Caire 1872, pl. 3.
Eg. Arch. & Lib., Varille Collection

Ses [*i.e.* de Mariette] jours et ses nuits furent employés à préparer l'inauguration du musée de Boulaq, et le jour même de mon arrivée au Caire, la besogne venait d'être terminée. À ce moment, le vice-roi n'avait pas encore exprimé le désir de visiter ce beau joyau de sa couronne. Tant de gens autour de lui parlaient avec mépris de ce ramassis de vieilleries sans intérêt, que peut être il avait fini par croire que son musée ne valait pas la peine qu'il se dérangeât afin d'aller le visiter. Disons tout de suite que j'ai peut-être eu le bonheur de le faire changer d'opinion sur ce sujet, car, le lendemain même de ma dernière visite au Palais, Mariette-Bey fut mandé par Son Altesse, afin de prendre jour pour l'inauguration du musée. Si je ne me suis pas trompé, et si j'ai pu contribuer à amener ce changement dans l'esprit du vice-roi, je déclare que j'en serai fier toute ma vie.

Venons maintenant à la description sommaire de cette inappréciable collection et du beau local qui la contient. [...] En résumé, le musée de Boulaq contenait, à l'heure où je l'ai visité, vingt-deux mille monuments catalogués, tous trouvés par Mariette, en quatre ans et demi de fouilles.

Afterwards, de Saulcy described his visit to the Khedive:

J'ai longuement parlé à Son Altesse de son musée de Boulaq, que j'ai visité dans la matinée, et dont je suis émerveillé. "Vous êtes plus avancé que moi, m'a dit le prince, j'attends que M. Mariette me permette à moi-même de voir ce musée". Il était facile d'apercevoir, dans ces paroles aigrelettes, le reflet de toutes les insinuations qui ont été répandues à foison dans l'esprit de Son Altesse à l'endroit de Mariette et du musée. J'ai donc saisi la balle au bond, et je lui ai dit qu'il se trompait sûrement en pensant que Mariette, le plus loyal comme le plus désintéressé de ses serviteurs, eût la pensée de lui faire attendre des permissions, au lieu d'attendre lui-même les ordres de son souverain ; que l'arrangement du musée n'avait été terminé que dans la nuit précédente ; que, pendant huit jours, Mariette avait fait antichambre pour lui annoncer ce résultat prochain, sans pouvoir parvenir jusqu'à sa personne, et que cela était bien suffisant pour lui causer un véritable chagrin ; que les dépenses faites pour l'installation de ce trésor inappréciable n'excédaient pas soixante mille francs, bien loin d'atteindre au chiffre de neuf cent mille francs, dont la calomnie avait essayé de faire peur à Son Altesse. Enfin, j'ai plaidé chaleureusement la cause de mon ami, si bien qu'Ismaïl-Pacha m'a paru singulièrement surpris de ce que mes appréciations différaient du blanc au noir de celles qu'on s'était plu à répandre dans son esprit. J'ai tout lieu de croire que, sur ce sujet, mes paroles n'ont pas été perdues.

(F. DE SAULCY, *Voyage en Terre-Sainte*, Paris 1865, pp. 31-42)

As a consequence, Ismail Pasha invited Mariette to the palace on October 23, 1863, to arrange his forthcoming visit to the museum, probably around that date.

The French archaeologist, presenting the new museum, underlined the temporariness of the setting, but he explained the nature and the aim of the institution:

Le Musée de Boulaq emprunte aux circonstances qui l'ont fait naître un caractère tout particulier. À part une bonne collection de petits objets achetés par S.A. Saïd-Pacha de M. Hubert, ancien Consul général d'Autriche, il est tout entier le produit de mes découvertes. Tandis qu'en Europe on ignore presque toujours la provenance de morceaux très importants, ici nous savons où le plus insignifiant fragment a été trouvé. La valeur de ce fait n'échappera à personne. [...] C'est un Musée organisé pour servir pratiquement l'égyptologie, et si les indifférents trouvaient à y blâmer l'introduction de quelques débris en apparence trop mutilés, je répondrais qu'il n'est pas un archéologue qui, avec moi, ne désirerait lui en voir encore davantage. [...] C'est de parti pris et après mûre réflexion que, dans l'emménagement intérieur des vitrines et des armoires, j'ai sacrifié au goût et cherché une certaine mise en scène qu'exclut ordinairement la froide régularité de nos Musées d'Europe. Les motifs qui m'ont guidé sont faciles à comprendre. Le Musée du Caire n'est pas seulement destiné aux voyageurs européens : dans l'intention du Vice-Roi, il doit être surtout accessible aux indigènes qu'il est chargé d'instruire dans l'histoire de leur

Colossal statue probably representing
Octavian Augustus as Pharaoh, from Karnak.
Garden of the Bulaq Museum (Cairo CG 701).
Photograph.
Eg. Arch. & Lib.

pays. Or, je ne médis pas la civilisation introduite sur les bords du Nil par la dynastie de Mehemet-Ali en prétendant que l'Égypte est encore trop jeune à la vie nouvelle qu'elle vient de recevoir, pour posséder un public facilement impressionnable aux choses de l'archéologie et de l'art. Il y a quelque temps, l'Égypte détruisait ses monuments ; elle les respecte aujourd'hui ; il faut que demain elle les aime. [...] Si le Musée ainsi arrangé plaît à ceux auxquels il est destiné, s'ils y reviennent souvent et en y revenant s'inoculent, sans le savoir, le goût de l'étude et, j'allais presque dire, l'amour des antiquités de l'Égypte, mon but sera atteint.

(A. MARIETTE, *Notice des principaux monuments exposés dans les galeries provisoires du Musée d'Antiquités Égyptiennes de S. A. le Vice-Roi à Boulaq*, Alexandrie 1864, pp. 4-8)

The new museum was regularly visited and often described by the travelers of the time. Arthur Rhoné's description, dated to the end of the 1870s, is particularly interesting:

La route en est assez longue et ne se fait qu'en voiture ou à baudets ; on tourne le dos au Mousky, on traverse l'Esbekyeh, on suit de longues avenues bordées de sycomores, à travers des terrains nus et vagues que l'on appelle des plantations ; à gauche, des traînées de boursouflures pierreuses indiquent des quartiers entiers tombés sur place au temps des croisades, peut-être. On trouve, au bout de tout cela, une petite place à l'entrée d'un vieux quartier, une grande porte dans un grand mur, et l'on entre : c'est le musée de Boulaq. Quelque chose de riant et de charmant apparaît tout d'abord : c'est une cour parsemée de vieux arbres, au fond de laquelle on voit couler le Nil au pied des fourrés de sycomores et de dattiers qui couvrent la rive opposée ; au delà, des plans successifs de verdure qui s'effacent et se perdent dans l'éloignement, puis les deux grandes pyramides de Gizeh, qui se confondent presque dans la même silhouette. À main gauche, dans la cour, s'élève l'habitation de M. Mariette et de sa famille ; à droite, la cour du musée, séparée de la première par une grille dont les piliers portent des moulages de ces petits sphinx qui, en 1850, mirent M. Mariette sur les traces du fameux *Serapeum* de Memphis. La chienne Bargoût, gardienne du musée et contemporaine de sa fondation, fait son kief sous un arbre, et Finette, la gazelle privée, bondit à travers la cour.
Le cabinet de travail de M. Mariette fait face au Nil, près de la porte d'entrée : Devéria nous y introduit, et nous trouvons le maître dans une grande pièce aux murs décorés de fresques à l'égyptienne, remplie de livres, d'antiquités, et d'où la vue plonge directement sur les ravissantes perspectives du Nil et de la région des Pyramides. Quelques années plus tôt, sous le règne de Saïd-pacha, nous n'aurions trouvé ici qu'un pâté de masures délabrées appartenant à la Compagnie du transit et servant de magasins depuis l'expédition française. La protection et les encouragements de Saïd et d'Ismaïl-pacha ont permis à M. Mariette d'y installer, dans des bâtiments provisoires, en peu de temps et sans frais trop considérables, le premier musée égyptien du monde.

(A. RHONÉ, *L'Égypte à petites journées. Études et souvenirs*, Paris 1877, pp. 62-63)

Another great traveler, Amelia Edwards, wrote in 1891:

Waiting the construction of a more suitable edifice, the present building gives temporary shelter to the collection. In the meanwhile, if there was nothing else to tempt the traveller to Cairo, the Boulak Museum would alone be worth the journey from Europe.

(A. EDWARDS, *A Thousand Miles up the Nile*, II, London 1877, p. 287)

The Nile floods were always a danger for the Bulaq Museum, located on the river bank, but the disastrous one of 1878 damaged it so seriously that Mariette spent the following two years restoring and rearranging it. He himself explained it to his friend Heinrich Brugsch in a letter now kept in the Milan Archives, dated March 9, 1880:

Il me semble qu'il y a bien longtemps que je ne vous ai écrit. Émile a dû vous en dire la cause. Nous venons de refaire le Musée tout entier à neuf, et je vous assure que ce n'était pas une petite besogne. J'en sors, pour moi, absolument fatigué et malade. [...] Heureusement notre peine n'a pas été perdue, et le nouveau Musée ne me fait en rien regretter l'ancien.

In an almost contemporaneous letter, dated April 4, 1880, deposited in the Milan Archives together with the collection of private correspondence of Giuseppe Botti "the First", the Italian scholar wrote:

Il Museo di Boulaq è qualche cosa di immenso: ora si scava fra la Sfinge e la gran Piramide.

Botti alludes to the newly reorganized Bulaq Collection, as well as to the resumption of Mariette's excavation activity and to the Antiquities Service, identified in Botti's letters with the museum, which housed the Director's office. Despite Mariette's hard work, that location was no longer suitable for a fast-growing collection.

Gaston Maspero and Victor Loret in Egypt
In January 1881, the young Egyptologist Victor Loret arrived in Egypt with his professor, Gaston Maspero, as a member of the just established Mission Archéologique Française.

On January 15 of the same year, Loret visited the Bulaq Museum for the first time. He movingly described the last days of Auguste Mariette's life in his diary, preserved today in the Milanese Archives:

Je suis allé ce matin prendre une connaissance générale du Musée de Boulaq. [...] Attenant au Musée se trouve la maison où Mr Mariette passe en ce moment très probablement les dernières heures de sa vie.

And on January 19 he wrote:

Je suis retourné cette après-midi au Musée de Boulaq mais non pas pour y travailler ; Mr Mariette est mort hier soir et on l'enterrait aujourd'hui. [...] Le cercueil, en sycomore, de forme égyptienne, très simple et fermé par des sceaux de cire rouge était exposé dans la salle principale du Musée, au pied du colosse de gran[it] gris assis, toujours de Ramsès II. [...] Et les dahabieh remontant paisiblement les eaux bleues du Nil! Et les habitants arabes de Boulaq réunis en foule devant leurs demeures pour voir une dernière fois leur hôte aimé de si longues années, qui, par son travail et son musée a fait connaître au monde entier le nom de leur pauvre village!

In addition to his diaries, in the Egyptological Archives of the University of Milan, there are a great number of notes, drawings, and reports by the scholar devoted to the Bulaq Museum. These materials not only list the many objects present in the collection in the first half of the 1880s, but also give details of their precise location in the rooms, the garden, and even in the storerooms.

The collocation of the objects inside the rooms is also of great importance from a museological point of view, because it inspired the spatial organization of all the other museums in Egypt.

At Mariette's death, the Milanese Luigi Vassalli – already Curator of the Museum since 1865 – was appointed to the directorship *ad interim*, and held this position from January 18 until February 7, 1881, as can be deduced from a note initialled by Gaston Maspero in the third volume of the *Journal d'Entrée* of the Cairo Museum.

Some months later, the discovery of the royal mummies in the first cache at Deir el-Bahri in July 1881 made it necessary to totally renovate the museum. The works started in November of the same year, under

I

Cercueils et momies.

1   Couvercle de cercueil en bois peint, au nom de la dame
     [hieroglyphs] (var. [hieroglyphs]). Bois.

2   Momie d'enfant, époque gréco romaine, recouverte d'un
     cartonnage doré d'imitation égyptienne, les deux bras repliés, le
     g. tenant un oiseau. La face, qui était rapportée, manque.

3 ⎫ Transp.   Cartonn. peint. Dame — [hieroglyphs]
  ⎬ au
4 ⎭ Musée.   —   —   — . [hieroglyphs]

5   Bois nu. Grand cercueil, figure peinte, légendes rares. Au
     milieu: [hieroglyphs] etc. En dedans
     l'épervier de l'Occident.

6 ⎫ Transp.   Cartonnage colorié de [hieroglyphs]   [hieroglyphs]
7 ⎬ au
8 ⎭ Musée   —   —   [hieroglyphs]   [hieroglyphs]
9

10-11   Deux pièces d'un grand cercueil rectangulaire:
     10. Pièce de côté. [hieroglyphs]
     11. Extremité; mêmes titres, [hieroglyphs] etc.   V. 12, 19.

12   Sarcophage en bois [hieroglyphs] de [hieroglyphs]
     [hieroglyphs] autres titres [hieroglyphs]
     [hieroglyphs]
     [hieroglyphs] Var. du nom: [hieroglyphs].   Comp. n° 19, 10-11.

13   Id. de [hieroglyphs] titres [hieroglyphs]
     [hieroglyphs]

14   Casque de momie, à figure dorée — sans nom.

15   Bois [hieroglyphs] de la dame [hieroglyphs] etc [hieroglyphs]
     [hieroglyphs] etc [hieroglyphs].

16   Bois [hieroglyphs] de la dame [hieroglyphs] ([hieroglyphs]
     [hieroglyphs]), fille de [hieroglyphs]
     etc [hieroglyphs].   Var. du nom. [hieroglyphs].

17   Bois [hieroglyphs] de la dame [hieroglyphs]
     Var. du nom du père: [hieroglyphs]

18   Bois. Cercueil en forme de momie de la dame [hieroglyphs]
     [hieroglyphs].

19   Bois. [hieroglyphs] de [hieroglyphs] etc
     [hieroglyphs]   Mêmes personnages que nos 12, 10, 11.

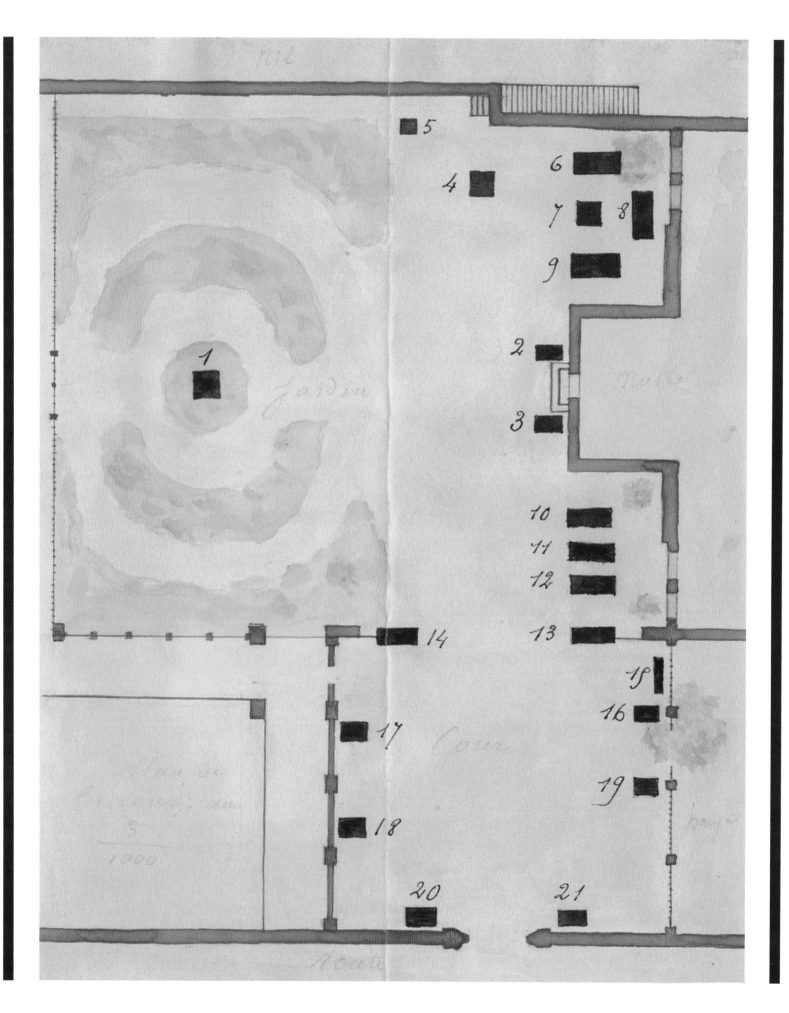

the directorship of Gaston Maspero, who followed Mariette as the head of the Antiquities Service and the Bulaq Museum. For five years, Maspero continued to study the objects of the collection and rearrange the rooms. His fervent activity can be traced through documents kept in the Archives, the letters that he regularly wrote to his wife Louise, and his publications. Among the latter, the guide of the museum, written at Bulaq in 1883 and issued in Paris in 1884, should be mentioned. In its introduction Maspero states:

Ce petit livre a été écrit pour l'usage des visiteurs ordinaires et non pour la commodité des Égyptologues : on y verra donc avant tout la description ou l'explication des monuments qui peuvent donner aux voyageurs la meilleure idée de l'art et de la civilisation égyptienne. Les gens du métier trouveront dans le cabinet du Directeur un catalogue sur fiches et une copie du Livre des fouilles qui leur permettront de découvrir la provenance et l'emplacement exacts de tous les objets conservés, soit dans les salles, soit dans les magasins du Musée.
(G. MASPERO, *Guide du visiteur du Musée de Boulaq*, Paris 1884, p. 3)

One of Maspero's assistants was Ahmed Kamal, the first Egyptian Egyptologist, who entered the museum as secretary-translator, but actually had many different tasks and worked with Émile Brugsch in clearing the aforementioned cache of mummies at Deir el-Bahri in 1881. The following year, Kamal opened a school of Egyptology at the museum, and some of his students, such as Mohamed Sha'ban and Hassan Hosni, became Inspectors of the Antiquities. However, Maspero decided to close the school in 1886, and to reallocate funds by creating new positions for the inspectors. This fact is mentioned in a letter that Maspero wrote to Louise on January 3, 1886:

J'ai pris un grand parti : j'ai demandé la suppression de l'école d'Ahmed Effendi. Je propose de créer cinq postes d'inspecteur nouveaux et deux de ghafir pour les élèves et de prendre les traitements sur les fonds alloués jadis à l'école. Les circonscriptions nouvelles seraient : 1° Assouan et Kom-Ombo ; 2° Le Fayoum ; 3° Pyramides de Gizéh et d'Abouroasch, celles de Saqqarah demeurant dans les mains de Tadious ; 4° Mansourah-Tanis ; 5° Saïs-Naucratis. [...] Je reprends en même temps l'idée de fonder un musée à Alexandrie, mais ce sera peut-être un peu difficile.
(É. David [éd.], *G. Maspero. Lettres d'Égypte*, Paris 2003, p. 104)

The Graeco-Roman Museum in Alexandria
and the Provincial Museums
In 1891, Giuseppe Botti "the First" reconsidered the idea of opening a museum devoted specifically to Graeco-Roman antiquities in Alexandria. The museum, under his directorship, opened in 1892 in a temporary location, and was then transferred to the present building in 1895.

In a letter dated October 31, 1893, deposited in the Milan Egyptological Archives, Botti wrote to his brother Carlo:

Non sono più al servizio del Governo Italiano, ma del Khédiwe [...] d'Egitto: lotto e lotto e faccio del mio meglio per fare onore al mio paese ed a quella buona Modena donde sono uscito e che non mi conosce più. [...] Non è l'Italia che ha fondato un Museo in Alessandria: è tuo fratello che l'ha creato, che lo dirige, che lo fa crescere con suo sacrificio.

Moreover, during the last years of the nineteenth century and in the first fifteen of the twentieth, Maspero and Kamal encouraged the national government and provincial authorities to establish regional museums of antiquities, in particular in Aswan, Asyut, Minia, and Tantah

Facing page:
Plan drawn by V. Loret of the court and the garden of the Bulaq Museum, with location of the monuments as arranged by A. Mariette.
Watercolor and manuscript, 1881.
Eg. Arch. & Lib., Loret Collection

Folowing pages:
Plan of the Bulaq Museum,
in G. MASPERO, *Guide du visiteur au Musée de Bulaq*,
[Le Caire] 1883.
Eg. Arch. & Lib., Edel Collection

G. Maspero (1846-1916). Photograph.
Eg. Arch. & Lib., Lacau Collection

Letter by G. Botti "the First" to his nephew
Antonio Botti, written from the Museum of Alexandria.
Manuscript, June 5, 1895.
Eg. Arch. & Lib., Botti Collection (long term deposit)

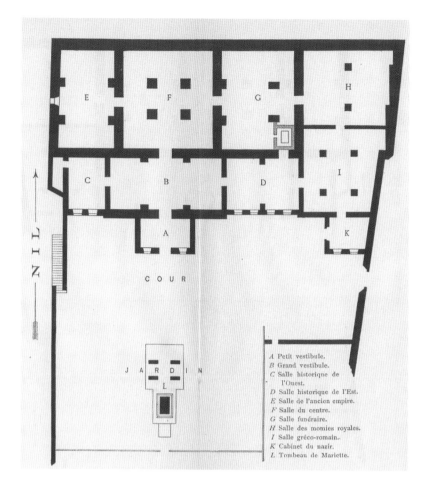

A Petit vestibule.
B Grand vestibule.
C Salle historique de
    l'Ouest.
D Salle historique de l'Est.
E Salle de l'ancien empire.
F Salle du centre.
G Salle funéraire.
H Salle des momies royales.
I Salle gréco-romain..
K Cabinet du nazir.
L Tombeau de Mariette.

non aveste, come me, mantenuto sinora intatto il vanto di gente onesta e di cuore lasciatoci dai nostri padri.

Mi parli di quel po' di nome che io ho nel mondo scienziato: tu non sai quello che mi costa. Io vivo scavando e sotterra cerco di rifare la storia di questa cara Alessandria che mi dà fama e pane per la famiglia. Tu credi che io abbia tre figli? Ne ho quattro: il primo si chiama e Museo Greco Romano di Alessandria ed è quello che amo di più, perché l'ho fatto io due volte ed è quello che mi costa di più. Molti giorni non vedo i miei figli che quando sono già addormentati!

Mi spiace, anzi ci spiace immensamente della malattia dello zio Don Giovanni e di quella di Carlo. Sono i soli avanzi legittimi della famiglia mia, e voglio vederli vivi fino al dì in che potrò abbracciarli di persona;

between 1912 and 1914. These collections were in addition to the Graeco-Roman Museum mentioned before, as well as to the Islamic (1884), Ethnographic (1895), Botanic (1898), Geologic (1904), Entomologic (1907), and Coptic (1908) Museums.

In another unpublished letter, dated February 22, 1899, from Botti to his nephew, the scholar writes:

Augusto [*i.e.* Botti's son] non è stato bene: io ho vegliato le intere notti e poi, per distrarmi, sono andato al Cairo, alle Piramidi, al Museo di Guizeh, al Giardino zoologico, al Museo Arabo … ed al nuovo Museo Geografico.

The Giza Museum
In 1887, the Egyptian Government had decided to temporarily transfer the collection of the Bulaq Museum to Ismail Pasha's palace at Giza, which was located in the park of the modern Cairo zoo, established in 1891. The building that had hosted the museum at Bulaq was then demolished in 1914.

The Giza Palace was imposing to look at but poorly constructed; it had been designed by Ambroise Baudry, among others architects. The Khedive had commissioned him in 1873. The palace was built by the company, owned by the Italian Giuseppe Garozzo, which would later build the new museum in the present Tahrir Square. The defects of the Giza Palace, and the fact that it was inadequate to be transformed into a museum, were underlined in a report by the Society for the Preservation of the Monuments of Ancient Egypt of June 1889, published five years later:

Considering the importance of the historical documents and unique works of art contained in the Boulak Museum, this committee, while recognising the urgent necessity of immediately finding another site for the collection […] regard with serious alarm the proposed removal of the museum to Ghizeh. The manifold dangers which would there threaten the collection arise from the fact of the palace of Ghizeh being constructed of combustible materials, which, if once ignited, would speedily reduce palace and collection to a heap of ashes without the chance of saving a single object: standing alone and near the desert, there would always be danger of robbers breaking in and carrying off the valuable series of jewellery and gold armaments. […] The committee, therefore, venture to hope that, before taking a step which is open to the foregoing objections, the Egyptian Government will reconsider the question.
(E.J. POYNTER ET AL., "The Ghizeh Museum", in *The Architect and Contract Reporter*, March 16, 1894, pp. 183-184)

Nevertheless, the antiquities were moved and installed there between the summer of 1889 and the winter of 1890, under the leadership of the new Director of the Antiquities Service, Eugène Grébaut, who held this position from 1886 to 1892. In the first guide of the new museum, issued in 1892, he writes:

Ce n'est pas sans regret que nous avons démonté les pièces rassemblées à Boulaq. Mariette, pendant vingt-cinq ans, M. Maspero, de 1881 à 1886, avaient travaillé à embellir l'ancien musée. […] Le musée de Boulaq était une œuvre d'art, dont les antiquités fournissaient les matériaux. On y voyait moins les objets exposés qu'un ensemble séduisant où se fondaient les détails, c'est-à-dire les monuments. Il faut avouer que le public avait vite traversé ces onze salles, garnies jusqu'au plafond, et en sortait sans que la plupart des pièces eussent attiré ses regards. […] Dès 1886, la circulation dans le musée était difficile. De nouveaux magasins furent aménagés à la suite des anciens, qui étaient remplis. En 1889, il n'y avait plus de place disponible, ni dans le musée, ni dans les magasins. Le produit des fouilles de cette année, resté dans la Haute-Égyp-

te sur un chaland et des barques, fut amené plus tard à Gizeh. […] Pendant que les Travaux publics préparaient le nouveau local, la Direction des musées, au cours de l'été de 1889, déménagea le musée et les magasins de Boulaq, puis, à mesure que les salles du palais de Gizeh lui furent livrés, y commença l'installation des antiquités.
([E. Grébaut, G. Daressy], *Musée de Gizeh. Notice sommaire des monuments exposés*, Le Caire 1892, pp. 3-7)

The Khedive Mohamed Tawfiq inaugurated the first forty-five rooms of the Giza Museum on January 12, 1890; in February, Mariette's tomb was moved there too from the garden of the Bulaq Museum. The following year, Ahmed Kamal was appointed Assistant Curator.

In November 1892, the new Khedive Abbas Pasha Hilmi II opened a further 46 rooms, in the presence of the new Director of the Antiquities Service, Jacques de Morgan. In the introduction to the second edition, de Morgan briefly described the new arrangement of the rooms:

Ces 91 salles renferment toutes les antiquités qui possède l'Égypte. Ces galeries sont, sans contredit, comme musée égyptologique, les plus riches et les mieux fournies qui soient dans le monde. Elles montrent la civilisation pharaonique dans les moindres détails, et, depuis les statues et les stèles royales de l'ancien empire jusqu'aux dernières œuvres d'art des chrétiens coptes, elles fournissent aux visiteurs toutes les manifestations du sentiment artistique des habitants de la vallée du Nil. Bien que très nombreuses, ces collections n'en sont pas moins appelées à prendre dans l'avenir une extension plus considérable encore ; chaque année, chaque mois elles s'enrichissent d'objets nouveaux et il est difficile de prévoir l'importance qu'il sera nécessaire de donner aux bâtiments destinés à renfermer des documents aussi nombreux. Quoi qu'il en soit, quelles que puissent être les découvertes, il est certain que dans quelques années, le palais de Gizeh lui-même sera devenu trop petit. […] La classification des antiquités dans le palais de Gizeh est faite suivant l'ordre chronologique aux étages inférieurs, et suivant la nature des objets aux étages supérieurs. […] Le musée se trouve donc naturellement divisé en deux parties : l'une comprenant les monuments volumineux et lourds qui sont exposés au rez-de-chaussée, et l'autre renfermant les objets petits ou légers qui ornent les salles du premier étage.
(J. de Morgan, "Avant-propos", in [P. Virey], *Notice des principaux monuments exposés au Musée de Gizeh*, Le Caire 1892, pp. XVIII-XXI)

Thanks to Sebah and other nineteenth century's photographers, it is possible to imagine how the objects were displayed, often in the same showcases or encircled by the same fences used at Bulaq. Since the museum was designed with the public in mind uppermost, the most important objects were accompanied by handwritten panels and often there were illustrative notes handwritten or cut from catalogues:

Du jour de l'ouverture du musée de Gizeh, l'Administration a fait coller sur les monuments les plus intéressants des descriptions tantôt manuscrites, tantôt découpées dans les catalogues du musée de Boulaq. Dans chaque salle le visiteur trouve des tableaux manuscrits qui appellent son attention sur les monuments les plus importants, les lui font connaître au moins sommairement.
([E. Grébaut, G. Daressy], *Musée de Gizeh. Notice sommaire des monuments exposés*, Le Caire 1892, p. 10)

The palace was beautiful, at least to look at, but many scholars did not appreciate it, as was the case with Wallis Budge, who wrote:

The massive mummies of Rameses II and other great kings looked sadly out of place in rooms with walls painted blue, and mouldings of salmon-pink picked out in gold, and ceiling decorated with panels, on which were painted Cupids, Venuses, etc.
(E.A. Wallis Budge, *The Nile: Notes for Travellers in Egypt*, London 1895⁴, p. 154)

Some years later, the journalist Henry Aubanel expressed many favourable opinions on the beautiful rooms opened by Victor Loret, who was Director of the Antiquities Service from 1897 until 1899:

Au musée di Ghizeh, dans le dédale du palais presque neuf et déjà caduc... Voici deux salles claires, pimpantes, donnant sur la gaîté du parc et battant neuf avec leurs vitrines fraîches. On les a ouvertes il y a trois jours et, s'ajoutant aux merveilleuses épaves de la vieille Égypte, y sont exposés tous les objets récemment découverts par M. Loret à Biban el Molouk, dans les tombeaux de Thotmès III et d'Aménophis II.
(H. AUBANEL, in *Le Journal Égyptien*, January 21, 1899, p. 1)

Most of the rooms had been decorated by the Italian painter Gaetano Lodi (see Chapter IV). But very soon the Giza Palace proved not large or safe enough to house the hundreds of objects that regularly arrived there following excavation campaigns. Moreover, its modernizing would have been so expensive, that the palace was demolished in 1902 and replaced by the still-existing faculty of engineering at Cairo University.

The International Competition for a New Egyptian Museum
In 1894 a committee of the Ministry of Public Works, which supervised the Antiquities Service, decided to open an international competition for the building of a new museum. Mariette's idea, already decreed by Ismail Pasha, of constructing either a monumental museum in Ezbekieh Square or a museum at the southern end of the island of Gezireh were abandoned for a location at Ismailiya (now Tahrir) Square. Here a large empty space was used as a cricket field by the English soldiers living in the nearby barracks. They were located in the south-western part of the area, approximately where the Palace of the Arab League and the former Nile Hilton Hotel stand today.

In a letter from the Director of the Antiquities Service, Jacques de Morgan, to the young Victor Loret, dated May 12, 1894 – and preserved today in the Loret Collection in the Archives of the University of Milan – we can read, among other things:

J'ai eu tant à faire que réellement je n'ai pas eu un instant à moi. J'ai été très pris par mes fouilles et aussi par une très grosse affaire, celle de la construction d'un musée neuf dans le Caire même. Ce transport des antiquités dans la ville était le rêve de Mariette. Le voilà enfin réalisé car nous avons obtenu trois millions pour ce monument. Mais que de courses, que de démarches que de projets. J'ai du mettre tout en mouvement la diplomatie de tous les pays d'Europe, trouver un terrain d'entente à ce sujet pour les plénipotentiaires français et anglais. J'ai employé deux ans à la poursuite de ce projet. Enfin c'est fini nous l'avons emporté et dans deux ou trois années tout le monde viendra facilement travailler dans nos galeries. Mais tout n'est pas fini car je suis en même temps chargé des projets définitifs et de la construction. J'aurai il est vrai bien des aides spéciaux mais ce n'en est pas moins un lourd fardeau en plus de mon administration, de mes fouilles et de nos publications.

The program of the competition, dated July 10, 1894, and signed by the Minister of Public Works Husayn Fakhry, was very detailed about the technical aspects expected for the new museum, but gave the architects great scope for the actual design:

Toute liberté est laissée aux architectes en ce qui concerne le style de la construction ; la décoration intérieure sera très simple. Avoir le plus de surface possible bien appropriée à l'exposition des collections, tel est le but principal

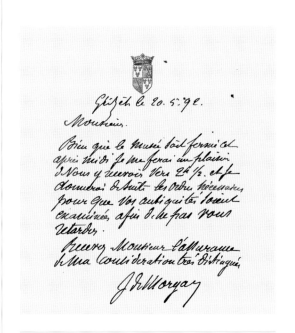

Letter by J. de Morgan to G.W. Fraser, written from the Giza Museum.
Manuscript, May 20, 1892.
Eg. Arch. & Lib., Fraser Collection

Facing page:
The main façade of the Giza Museum.
Photograph by J.P. Sebah.
Eg. Arch. & Lib., Private Collection (long term deposit)

Gallery 26 on the ground floor of the Giza Museum.
Photograph by J.P. Sebah.
Eg. Arch. & Lib., Private Collection (long term deposit)

qu'on doit se proposer, sans perdre de vue toutefois le caractère imposant qui convient à un édifice destiné à contenir les trésors antiques de la vieille Égypte.
(Gouvernement Egyptien, *Programme du concours pour l'érection d'un musée des antiquités égyptiennes au Caire*, Le Caire 1894, p. 11)

Among the seventy-three competition entries on show at Abdin Palace from March 14 till April 15, 1895, twenty-three came from Italy, sixteen from France, sixteen from England, and a few from the Austro-Hungarian Empire, Germany, North America, Bosnia, Holland, Greece, Syria, Malta, and obviously Egypt. Many were in "Egyptianizing" style, arranged as temples or pyramids, others were either too expensive, or too big, or too small, or didn't respect the lighting instructions. In the end, the neoclassical-style museum designed by the French architect Marcel Dourgnon was chosen. Many plates relating to this project are preserved in the archives of the Egyptian Museum in Tahrir Square, Cairo, and are partially published in the volume issued only in Arabic in 2002 for the centenary celebration of the museum. They were also shown on the occasion of the exhibition *The History of the Cairo Museum*, organized by the Chair of Egyptology of the University of Milan and the Egyptian Museum in Cairo in 2008-09.

Jacques de Morgan wholeheartedly agreed with this choice, while others were critical, such as the Italian architect Ernesto Basile, who harshly criticized the submissions on show at Abdin Palace in a booklet published in Cairo and dated March 19, 1895. He was bitterly disappointed since no Italian projects had been selected. According to the Italian press of the time in Egypt, this was because Basile, who should have been part of the competition's committee, arrived from Italy too late, when the awarding of prize giving had already been completed. Nevertheless, he expressed a hazy but quite positive opinion about Dourgnon's entry, number 49, at least before knowing the final verdict:

La superficie coperta da questo progetto è del 50% superiore alla richiesta: nel caso di un probabile ingrandimento tutta l'area disponibile sarebbe occupata. Questo è un progetto dei più studiati nelle piante e nelle facciate, ma è uno dei tanti che sono fuori concorso perché hanno voluto fare troppo ed hanno trattato il programma come meglio hanno voluto. Il progetto è in uno stile classico dei più imponenti, e chi lo studiò, è una mente superiore di certo, ma per sua disgrazia il Governo Egiziano non dispone di sufficienti mezzi per praticamente encomiare tanto talento.

But at the end of his critical review of the submissions, after the last sentence, he added:

Al momento di mettere in macchina l'opuscolo, ci viene comunicato il verdetto della commissione esaminatrice, verdetto che non è altro che una partigianeria sfacciata, o frutto di assoluta incompetenza nei membri della giuria. Questo giudizio [è] degno dei tempi preistorici.
(E. B[ASILE], *Museo Egiziano. Rivista critica dei progetti esposti al concorso*, Cairo 1895, pp. 15-16)

The Cairo Italian newspaper *L'Imparziale*, which widely covered the competition when it was on, published some articles, between March and April 1895, with comments on the various entries, including Dourgnon's one:

Il numero 49 è in istile barocco con un'impronta di moderno niente indovinata e delle facce laterali si può addirittura dire che sono di concezione artistica molto meschina: lo stesso dicasi di quelle due orecchie che terminano i fianchi della facciata e che l'autore riserverebbe al direttore e agli uffici e che dan-

Offert au deuxième Congrès International d'Archéologie par Karl Bædeker

LE CAIRE
(MAṢR EL-ḲÂHIRA)
1:12.300

Mètres
Yards
Abréviations:
D.=Derb, H.=Hara, M.=Mosquée
S.=Souk, Sh.=Shâria.
Tramways.

Les bâtiments où auront lieu les
séances du Congrès sont marqués
en rouge

GÉZIRET BEDRÂN

BOÛLÂḲ

QUARTIER TEWFIKIYEH

ISMAÏLÎYEH

QUARTIER EL-EZBEKIYEH

QUARTIER ROSETTI

Khân el-Khalîli

Musée égyptien

Hôpital militaire anglais

KAṢR EN-NÎL
Champ
Casernes de Mars

Grand Pont
de Kaṣr en-Nîl
Université

KAṢR ED-DOUBÂRA
Palais

LE NIL

KAṢR EL-AINI

GÉZIRET RODA

Midân Abdîn
Palais Abdîn

EL-ḤILMÎYEH

Mosquée Ibn Touloun

CITADELLE
Mohammed Ali

Tombeaux des Mamelouks

Cimetière mahométan

Tombeaux des Khalifes

Petit bras du Nil

Gravé et imprimé par Wagner & Debes, Leipzig.

no l'idea delle appendici che si sogliono aggiungere ai ristoranti di campagna. [...] Indovinatissima invece è la disposizione della biblioteca e della sala di vendita e l'illuminazione è pure bene ottenuta con aperture di fianco ai lucernari oppure con vetrate inclinate in un senso, quantunque queste non intercetterebbero i raggi solari.

(Anonymous, "Concorso Internazionale per un museo di antichità egiziane da erigersi in Cairo. Appunti e impressioni", VI, in *L'Imparziale* IV/86-87, March 27-28, 1895, p. 2)

The Construction and Opening of the New Museum

The foundation stone of the museum was laid on April 1, 1897, in the presence of the Khedive Abbas Hilmi II, Jacques de Morgan, other authorities, and the architect Marcel Dourgnon. Meanwhile, in December 1896, Giuseppe Garozzo, the most famous building contractor working in Egypt at that time, together with another Italian business man, Francesco Zaffrani, was charged of the construction that took four years, from 1897 until 1901.

Reinforced concrete works, like the cupola overhanging the entrance hall was made by another company owned by an Italian business man, Nicola Marciano, who had collaborated with Garozzo on other important buildings in Cairo, such as part of the Abdin Palace and Shepheard's Hotel.

The works proceeded in a very chaotic way, as can be deduced from archive documents and the press of the time, and posed many problems to the Directors of the Antiquities Service who succeeded de Morgan, first Victor Loret and then Gaston Maspero. While the latter was holding this position, the museum was finally opened to the public.

Moving five thousand wooden crates of antiquities from Giza to the new museum in the city center was a difficult operation, directed by Gaston Maspero and his assistant Alessandro Barsanti. At the end of 1899 those wooden crates had been made by the carpenter Mohamed Issa. Two years later, in December 1901, the showcases were moved from Giza and installed inside the new rooms. In mid February 1902, the first 272 sarcophagi were transported, and then, starting in the beginning of March, the smaller objects.

Besides Émile Brugsch, Daressy and von Bissing, the young Pierre Lacau collaborated on the transfer of the objects too. He was beginning his activity in Egypt, as shown by his personal archives, preserved today at the University of Milan.

The transportation of the antiquities went on until July 13, 1902. At this date, Mariette's sarcophagus, designed by Ambroise Baudry was also moved for the second time. The huge gates from the Giza Palace designed by the same architect were tranferred too, and were shared among the new museum, the Abdin Palace, and the Parliament.

At the beginning of September, the museum began to be visited by scholars and foreigners passing through Cairo. Finally, on November 15, 1902, it was officially opened.

The Museum's Sale Room

The creation of a museum totally devoted to Egyptian antiquities and the regulation for export of the objects – on which Loret had written a detailed report, unpublished and preserved today in Milan, and followed by a law proposal written by Gaston Maspero in 1902 and issued in 1912 – did not stop antiquities leaving the country. The law proposal in fact was never applied.

Facing page:
The court in front of the Egyptian Museum in Cairo, with the iron fence designed by A. Baudry previously at the Giza Palace. The English barracks can be seen in the background. Photograph.
Eg. Arch. & Lib., Varille Collection

The neoclassical façade of the Egyptian Museum in Cairo, designed by M. Dourgnon. Photograph.
Eg. Arch. & Lib., Varille Collection

Up until the middle of the 1970s, there was a room inside the museum – first in Giza and then in the one in the center of Cairo – devoted to the sale of the objects already widely present in the collection. This can be deduced from many sources, including the museum guides, the construction program of the new museum, or the inspector's excavation journals of the Antiquities Service, like Quibell's ones in Milan today. In these notebooks, one can often read the list of the objects that could be sent to the Sale Room.

Other information can be guessed from the registers of acquisition belonging to Egyptian museums all over the world. In the Sale Room's register, the purchaser was usually mentioned beside the objects; this could be a private or a foreign museum, which was generally European, Russian, or American. The register was often consulted, from the 1950s, by Bernard V. Bothmer, who took pictures of some of the pages, which are now preserved in the Egyptological Archives of the University of Milan.

At the Giza Museum, the Sale Room was located on the ground floor in room 91, accessible directly from outside, as can be seen in a beautiful photograph preserved in the Lacau Collection in Milan, as well as in the plan of the museum. In the new museum in the center of Cairo, instead, the Sale Room was accessible from the western entrance, which leads today to the offices of the Directorate. Ancient objects could also be bought from the many antiquities' sellers, official or improvised, working mostly in Cairo, Alexandria, and Luxor. All the sales were stopped in the 1970s and were strictly regulated by law.

From the First Renovation of the Museum to New Projects
Only a few years after its construction, the new building of the Cairo Museum revealed the first of its structural problems. The roof needed fixing:

Lorsque, du 13 février au 13 juillet 1902, M. Maspero transporta la collection égyptienne de Gizéh au Caire dans l'édifice construit spécialement au Kasr-en-Nil pour la recevoir, sa lourde tâche ne fut point terminée : il fallait classer les objets par ordre de matières et de dates, aménager les salles d'exposition et la bibliothèque, cataloguer les séries scientifiquement et faire connaître le sens des plus importantes au grand public, toutes choses assez difficiles car [...] l'exécution qui en avait eu lieu de 1897 à 1902 avait été entachée de malfaçons telles que l'on dut refaire presque immédiatement, de 1907 à 1915, toutes les terrasses en ciment armé et, par conséquent, modifier sans cesse à l'intérieur la disposition des salles.
(G. MASPERO, "Les Études Égyptologiques", in AA.VV., *Exposition Universelle et Internationale de San Francisco. La Science française*, II, Paris 1915, p. 24)

In 1925 an important proposal for the reconstruction of the museum to include a research center and a library was presented to King Fuad I by the American Egyptologist James Henry Breasted. According to this proposal, the management of antiquities and excavations should have been controlled by a foundation. The project, which should have been financed by John D. Rockefeller Jr. with ten million dollars – equivalent to hundred million today – seems to have been strongly supported by his daughter, Abigail "Abby" Rockefeller Mauzé "Babs", who was an Egyptology enthusiast. Breasted offered and dedicated some of his volumes to her between 1916 and 1925, which later entered William Kelly Simpson's library. Babs' daughter, Marilyn Rockefeller Milton, married this famous American Egyptologist, who recently offered his personal scientific correspondence and some materials from his archives to the University of Milan. His library, instead, was bought by a private foundation. The project, which in practise excluded Egyptians from the management of the antiquities and gave decisional power to the Americans and English, had been refused by local authorities, probably also under pressure from Pierre Lacau, then the Director of the Antiquities Service.

At present, research into his personal archives, which have recently been deposited in the University of Milan, is under development to find out what the reactions of the French Egyptologist were to Breasted's proposal, and this research will be extended to the portion of his archives preserved at the Institut de France.

Another interesting project to extend the Egyptian Museum into a large "city of museums" dates back to 1937, when the English barracks should have been demolished. It was proposed by Ludwig Borchardt and signed by his assistant Otto Königsberger, but it was soon abandoned because of Borchardt's age, Königsberger's health problems, and the outbreak of the Second World War.

In 1970-71, the Egyptian architect Ahmed Abd el Hamid was asked by the Minister of Culture to design the enlargement of the museum with a new wing, but the project was stopped in May 1971 with the change of Minister. Other partial renovation works, interesting special sections or rooms – such as the Fourth Dynasty and Hetepheres' Room on the ground floor, or the Prehistory Hall, the Royal mummies' Rooms, and the Animal mummies' Room on the first floor – were accomplished in the last twenty years.

In the 1990s, the decision was finally taken to lighten the vast collection at the Egyptian Museum in Cairo, not only by creating and enlarging many provincial museums, but also by building two new big museums in Cairo, the GEM (Grand Egyptian Museum) in the Giza area in front of the Great Pyramids, and the National Museum of Egyptian Civilization in the Fustat area. The sharing of the antiquities among the various museums will be followed by the complete renovation of the historical Museum in Tahir. While choosing which antiquities should be moved from one museum to another, the objects are studied and catalogued, with the support of advanced computer systems. The historical series of the *Catalogue Général des antiquités égyptiennes du Musée du Caire* is on-going. Its origin goes back to 1897, when a group of scholars lead by Ludwig Borchardt conceived of a huge organic but functional plan, aimed at the scientific publication of all the objects in the museum, grouped by category, period, or provenance.

The *Catalogue Général* counts now more than one hundred volumes. Nevertheless, several categories of objects still require specific research, even if they have already been assigned an accession number in the *Catalogue Général*, whereas other items are included in unpublished manuscripts left by authors and frequently deposited in the Archives of the Museum.

Following pages:
p. 30. Some of the first members of the International Cairo Catalogue Commission outside the Giza Museum: (left to right) F.W. von Bissing, J.E. Quibell, É.G. Chassinat, G.A. Reisner and L. Borchardt. Photograph, 1898 or 1899.
Eg. Arch. & Lib., Lacau Collection

p. 31. (Left to right) É. Brugsch, F.W. von Bissing and P. Lacau on the balcony of the Giza Museum. The entrance to the Sale Room can be seen on the ground level. Photograph, March 12, 1898.
Eg. Arch. & Lib., Lacau Collection

p. 32. Plan of the ground floor of the Giza Museum, in J. DE MORGAN, *Notice des principaux monuments exposés au Musée de Gizeh*, Le Caire 1892.
Eg. Arch. & Lib., Varille Collection

J. DE MORGAN, *Notice des principaux monuments exposés au Musée de Gizeh*, Le Caire 1892, p. 334, with mention of the Sale Room, numbered 91.
Eg. Arch. & Lib., Varille Collection

p. 33. Plan of the Egyptian Museum in Cairo, in K. BAEDEKER, *Égypte et Soudan: Manuel du Voyageur*, Leipzig-Paris 1908⁵.
Eg. Arch. & Lib., Varille Collection

pp. 34-35. Page from a notebook concerning J.E. Quibell's excavations at Saqqara, with mention of the Sale Room of the Egyptian Museum in Cairo. Manuscript, 1907-1910.
Eg. Arch. & Lib., Quibell Collection

pp. 36-37. Two pages from the Register of the Sale Room of the Egyptian Museum in Cairo. Photograph.
Eg. Arch. & Lib., Bothmer Collection

p. 38. The Stone Sarcophagi Hall, on the ground floor of the Egyptian Museum in Cairo. Photograph, probably 1913.
Eg. Arch. & Lib., Varille Collection

Showcases on the first floor of the Egyptian Museum in Cairo. Photograph, probably 1913.
Eg. Arch. & Lib., Varille Collection

p. 39. View on the first floor of the Egyptian Museum in Cairo. Photograph, probably 1913.
Eg. Arch. & Lib., Varille Collection

pp. 40-41. The staff of the Service des Antiquités under the direction of P. Lacau. Photograph, explanatory flimsy paper and corresponding names, March 31, 1936.
Eg. Arch. & Lib., Lacau Collection

p. 42. Poster of the exhibition *The History of the Cairo Museum*, organized in Cairo in 2008 by the Chair of Egyptology of the University of Milan and the Direction of the Cairo Museum.
Eg. Arch. & Lib.

v. Bissing   J.E. Quibell   E Chassinat   Reisner.   Borchardt.

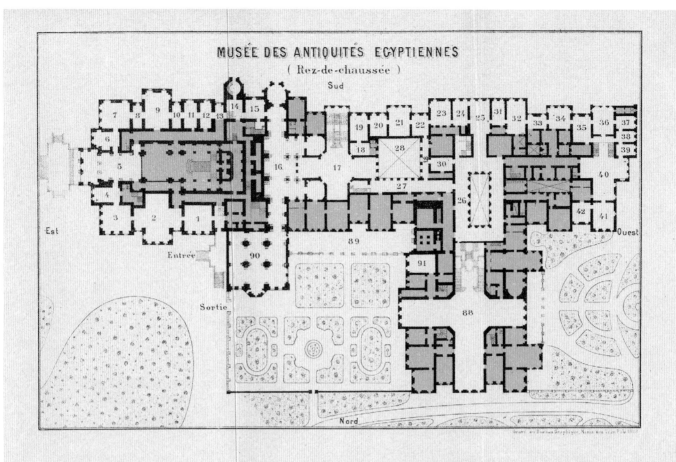

MUSÉE DES ANTIQUITÉS EGYPTIENNES
(Rez-de-chaussée)

1277 -- Bois — Haut. 2ᵐ,19. — Époque ptolémaïque
— *Akhmim*.

Cercueil en bois pesant, sans peinture ; le visage seul
est doré et les yeux sont rapportés. Le défunt avait été
deuxième prophète de Min (ou Khem).

Un grand nombre d'autres cercueils garnissent
les murs de la salle 87. Nous ne pouvons les dé-
crire en détail; les uns proviennent des sépultures
des prêtres de Mentou (ou Month), à Thèbes
(Gournah) et sont surtout de l'époque saïte ; d'autres proviennent d'Akhmim et sont généralement
contemporains des Ptolémées.

————

Salle 88 (Monuments funéraires).

En sortant de la salle 87, le visiteur repasse sur
le palier où il a vu tout à l'heure le couvercle du
cercueil de la reine Ahhotpou I (N. 1251), et
arrive, en descendant l'escalier, dans la grande
salle des monuments funéraires du rez-de-chaussée
(salle 88). C'est la dernière salle à visiter. (Les nu-
méros 89, 90 et 91 s'appliquent à des galeries
extérieures contenant des monuments de moindre
intérêt et à la salle des ventes.)

MUSÉE DES ANTIQUITÉS ÉGYPTIENNES

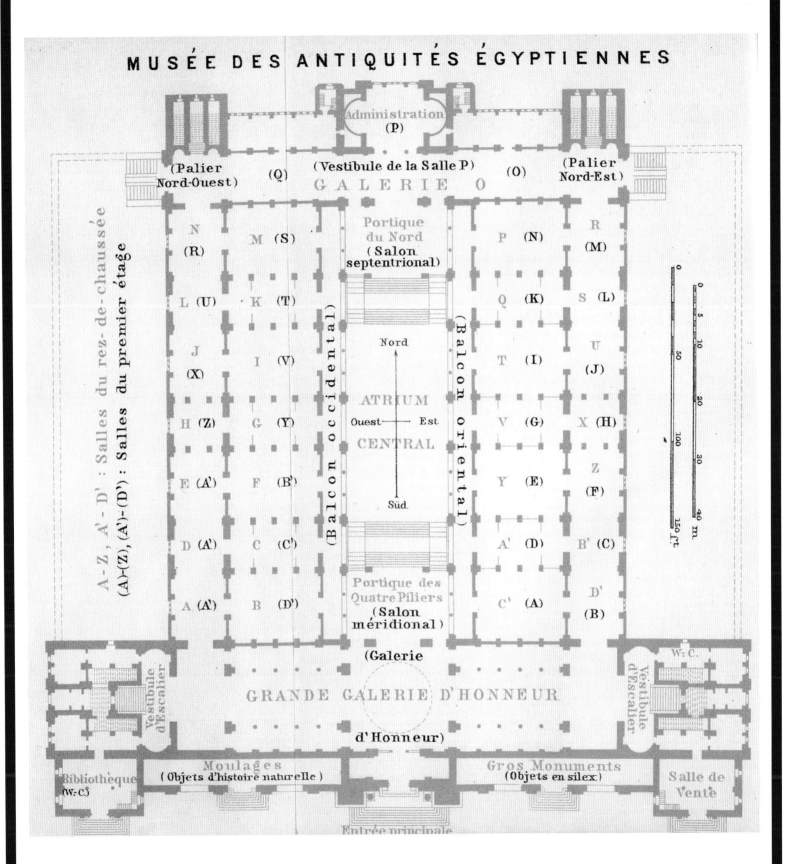

Administration
(P)

(Palier Nord-Ouest)   (Q)   (Vestibule de la Salle P)   (O)   (Palier Nord-Est)

GALERIE O

A - Z, A' - D' : Salles du rez-de-chaussée
(A)-(Z), (A')-(D') : Salles du premier étage

N (R)   M (S)   Portique du Nord (Salon septentrional)   P (N)   R (M)

L (U)   K (T)   Q (K)   S (L)

J (X)   I (V)   T (I)   U (J)

(Balcon occidental)   Nord   ATRIUM   (Balcon oriental)

H (Z)   G (Y)   Ouest — Est   V (G)   X (H)   Z (F)

CENTRAL

E (A')   F (B')   Süd   Y (E)   (F)

D (A')   C (C')   A' (D)   B' (C)

A (A')   B (D')   Portique des Quatre Piliers (Salon méridional)   C' (A)   D' (B)

(Galerie

GRANDE GALERIE D'HONNEUR

d'Honneur)

Vestibule d'Escalier   W. C.   Vestibule d'Escalier

Bibliothèque (W. C.)   Moulages (Objets d'histoire naturelle)   Gros Monuments (Objets en silex)   Salle de Vente

Entrée principale

Stores left over from last season
packed by Aly abdel Azim, sent
for Salle de Vente.

		Size	Card	Date sent	Letter
15/8	Inscr 𓏏𓎡𓆓 etc.	14	701	13 May 08	264
	2 moulds of Rekhyt.	9			
	Inscr in ink on marble (copied by Sethe) Carney				
	Small Saite statue	16			
	Fine ls head from Teta	21			
	2 frags of boat scene bigger	28	920		
	Alab face	20 wdi	356		
	Stela (𓏏𓆓𓃀 etc)	30 h.	361		
	Small apex stela.	13 b	726		
	Marble frag Jonah & whale	12	780		
	Marble font in 3 frags.				264
9.8.	5 Coptic capitals, mostly screen		24	407	
	Floral ornam				
	OK scene 𓉐 𓂧𓄿 etc				
	𓂋𓏌𓅓𓏏 seated before table				
	2 frags stela 𓆓𓏏𓄿 (x li).				
	Frag. of 𓊽𓏏𓏤𓏥				
	Stela 𓏏𓉐𓏏𓆓𓆓 2 pieces				
	Inscr. with ☉ 𓂀 𓂧				
	XIXth Dyn scene colᵈ RaTum.				
	Top xth Dyn stela — Girls offerings				
	Frag of 𓏏𓏤𓏏𓉐𓆓𓆓				

Print. Govt. Mess. A. 1943-20 500

مقاييس الأثر DIMENSIONS	المادة المصنوع منها MATERIAL	وصف الأثر DESCRIPTION	موضع الأثر POSITION	رقم مسلسل NUMBER
٢٦ سم	جرانيت أسود	تمثال لنصف رجل بمصري (؟)	٦٠٩ - بر/٢/٦٥ C٠.٠٢٤	١٢
٢٩ سم	كوارتز	تمثال لنصف لرجل	٦٠٩ - بر/٢/٦٥ C٠.٠٢٤	١٣
٢٢٨ ٣٤	حجر جيري	....	C٤٩٩ - ٠٢/...	١٤
٩٥٠ ٦٠	حجر جيري	.... haocoan	C٠.٠٦ - ٠٢/٥/٩	١٥
٢٥٠ ٦٦ ٥٠	حجر جيري	....	C٤٩٣ - ٠٢/٤/٦٥	١٦
طول: ٣٣ ١١	جرانيت أسود	تمثال لسيدة (إيزيس)	C٤٩٧ - ٠٢/٤/٦٥	١٧
٢٥ ١٧	رخام	رأس رخام لرجل	C٠.٢ - ٠٢/٥/٩	١٨
٤٢	جرانيت أسود	....	٠٢/٥/١٣ (.........) ٢-١-١١......	١٩
طول: ٢٥٦ ٦٥	حجر جيري	....	٠٢/٥/١٣	٢٠
٤٧٫٥ ٤٢	حجر جيري	....	C٠١١ - ٠٢/٥/١٣	٢١
٢٥	رخام	....	C٠١٥ - ١٩/٥/٩	٢٢
٢٦	رخام	....	C٠١٦ - ١٩/٥/٩	٢٣
٢٦	جرانيت أسود رخام أحمر	....	C٠٢٢ - ٠٩/٦/٦	٢٤

Provenance	Remarks ملاحظات عامة	Photograph صورة الأثر أو رسمه
	Endre Ungar ; Mexico.	
	" " "	
	Mlle Bissigt , Genève , Suisse.	
	M. T. de Suppan : Suisse.	
	Thomas Morgan ;	
	Koffler, Lucerne ; Suisse.	
	= Leiden F 1960/3, 1	
	M. Jérome Eisenberg ; New-York ; U.S.A	
	Mr D. Endre Ungar ; Mexico.	
	" " " " "	
	M. Joseph Kairz ; Germany.	
	W. B. Tucker ; Rome Italie.	

1.	Abdel Halim Hilmi Eff.	Dessinateur
2.	Abdel Sadek Mahmoud Eff.	Chauffeur
3.	Mahmoud Moukhtar Eff.	Préposé à la Porte d'Entrée
4.	Youssef Eff. Khafaga	Dessinateur
5.	Mohamed Eff. Ibrahim	Aide-Ingénieur
6.	Mohamed Eff. El-Mansouri	Aide-Photographe
7.	Ahmed Eff. El-Lakkani	Secrétaire Inspect. Basse-Egypte
8.	Ibrahim Eff. Kamel	Comptable
9.	Ragai Eff. Kallini	"
10.	Benjamin Eff. Louka	Sous-Chef. Comptable
11.	Moubarak Eff. Bichara	Directeur Administratif
12.	Mahmoud Eff. Hamza	Conservateur-adjoint Musée
13.	M. Philippe Lauer	Architecte à Saqqarah
14.	M. Gustave Jéquier	Archéologue à Saqqarah
15.	M. Octave Guéraud	Conservateur-adjoint Musée
16.	M. Henri Gauthier	Secrétaire Général
17.	M. Pierre Lacau	Directeur Général
18.	M. Reginald Engelbach	Conservateur en Chef du Musée
19.	M. Guy Brunton	Conservateur-adjoint du Musée
20.	M. W. B. Emery	Archéologue à Saqqarah
21.	Tewfik Eff. Boulos	Inspecteur en Chef Moyen-Egypte
22.	M. Louis Lanzel	Chef Atelier de Moulage
23.	M. Henri Ainut	Sous-Directeur Administratif
24.	Mohanam Eff. Kamal	⎫
25.	Maurice Eff. Raphaël	⎬ Conservateurs-adjoints Musée
26.	Abdel Hadi Eff. Hamada	⎭
27.	Mikias Eff. Fam	Inspecteur Sohag
28.	Kamal Eff. Hussein	Chef Rédacteur-Arabe
29.	Nasrallah Eff. Gohran	Nazer du Musée
30.	Hakim Eff. Abou-Seif	Inspecteur Bain. Saqqarah
31	Boutros Eff. Awad	Chef Archiviste
32	Riskallah Eff. Mahramallah	Archéologue à Saqqarah
33	Abdel Moneim Eff. Mohamed	Chef Comptable
34	Antoun Eff. Zikri	Bibliothécaire
35	Enani Eff. Ismaïl	Vérificateur-Comptable
36	Mohamed Eff. Hassanein	Préposé à la Salle de Vente
37	Moussa Eff. Ghaleb	Comptable
38	Nasri Eff. Nasri	Traducteur
39	Ismaïl Eff. Chehab	Chef-Photographe
40	Kamel Eff. El-Miniawi	Archiviste
41	Mohamed Eff. Hassan	"
42	Michel Eff. Zayat	Comptable
43	Sadek Eff. Ahmed	"
44	Fahmi Eff. Moh. Ali	"
45	Sabri Eff. Sebeh	Rédacteur-Traducteur
46	Youssef Eff. Osman	Comptable
47	Zaki Eff. Youssef Saad	Archéologue à Saqqarah
49.	Ahmed Eff. Saad	Chef Atelier de Peinture
50.	Abdel Baki Eff. Youssef	Inspecteur d'Edfou
51.	Anwar Eff. Rouchdi	Comptable
52.	Sadek Eff. Fanous	Secrétaire du Nazir
53.	Labib Eff. Habachi	Inspecteur de Louxor
54.	Ramzi Eff. Ghali	Archiviste
55	Raymond Eff. Francis	Rédacteur-Traducteur
57	Boutros Eff. Cassab	"
58	Harmos Eff. Baskharon	Menuisier
59	Chafik Eff. Nasri	Bureau du Personnel
60	Michel Eff. Cassab	Chef-Traducteur-Rédacteur Européen
61	Mohamed Eff. Abdel Hakim	Magasinier
62	Hussein Eff. Ragal	Restaurateur
63	Hamed Eff. Sobh	Chef-Menuisier
64	Mahmoud Eff. Mohamed	"
66.	Mahmoud Abdel Rahim	Chef Ferrache du Musée
72.	Abou Zeid El-Sonefi	Saï de M. le Directeur Général

48-56-65-67 à 71, 73 à 79 - Ferraches.
80-81. Jardiniers

31 Mars 1936

من موظفي المصرية الى جناب
مسيو هـ ؟ بيير لا...
١٩٣٦ (مارس)

Souvenir
...senté à Monsieur
...Pierre Lacau
...les fonctionnaires
...u Service Des
...ntiquités Egyptiennes
...aire, le 31 Mars 1936

Chalab
1936

70 71 72 73 74 75 76 77 78 79 80
54 55 56 57 58 59 60 81
61 62 63 64 65 66 67 68 69
40 41 42 43 44 45 46 47 48 49 50 51 52 53
24 25 26 27 28 29 30 31 32 33 34 35 36 37 38 39
11 12 13 14 15 16 17 18 19 20 21 22 23
1 2 3 4 5 6 7 8 9 10

The History
of the
Egyptian Museum

Egyptian Museum in Cairo

October 19 - November 19, 2008

Photographers in Egypt 1850-1950

Laura Marucchi, Patrizia Piacentini

VUE PERSPECTIVE INTÉRIEURE COLORIÉE DU TEMPLE DE L'OUEST.

II. *Photographers in Egypt 1850-1950*

Laura Marucchi, Patrizia Piacentini

Photography was officially born on 19 August 1839, when François Arago presented the daguerreotype, invented by Louis Jacques Mandé Daguerre, to the Académie des Sciences in Paris. On this occasion, Arago suggested using this new technique in Egypt for documentary purposes. A few months later, the Parisian optician, Noël Paymal Lerebours, sent the famous painter Horace Vernet and his nephew Frédéric Goupil-Fesquet to the Valley of the Nile, where they were joined by the photographer Gaspard-Pierre-Gustave Joly de Lotbinière. The purpose of the trip was to produce for publication the first daguerreotypes of Egyptian views and monuments. This turned out to be impossible, however, because the daguerreotype is a one-off and cannot be duplicated. It is a direct positive image, exposed on a very delicate copper plate coated with a layer of silver and sensitized with iodine vapour.

Nevertheless, between 1841 and 1843, Lerebours managed to publish the *Excursions Daguerriennes*, a collection of lithographs and watercolors based on the first photographs of Egypt and the Near East. At the same time, other collections were appearing such as *Panorama d'Égypte et de Nubie*, published in 1841 by Hector Horeau and inspired by the daguerreotypes of Joly de Lotbinière. Various other daguerreotypists were also working in Egypt during this period. All of these publications immediately became very popular, increasing the public's interest in photography and enhancing Egypt's appeal.

At the beginning of the nineteenth century, scholars, artists, and adventurers had already turned their attention to the Valley of the Nile, thanks to important publications such as the monumental *Description de l'Égypte*, produced by the *savants* who accompanied Napoleon to Egypt. These young scholars arrived in Egypt in 1798 where they remained until 1801. During this time they accurately recorded and described every aspect of the country, both ancient and modern. In addition, highly successful events, including the exhibition in Piccadilly, London, in 1821 and the antiquities brought to light by Giovanni Battista Belzoni, fuelled the already widespread Egyptomania. Other artistic productions, such as lithographs and watercolors representing Egyptian monuments and landscapes, like those by Edward William Lane and David Roberts, kept the interest in oriental wonders alive.

The first archaeological expeditions date back to the first half of the nineteenth century. The main objective of the Franco-Tuscan expedition led by Jean François Champollion and Ippolito Rosellini in 1828-29 and the Prussian one headed by Richard Lepsius in 1842-45 was to discover, study, and reproduce bas-reliefs and inscriptions on tombs and monuments. As a result, during the nineteenth century the Valley of the Nile became one of the compulsory stopping places in the Grand Tour of the East for rich Europeans and Americans as well as a place often visited by kings and princes during their travels.

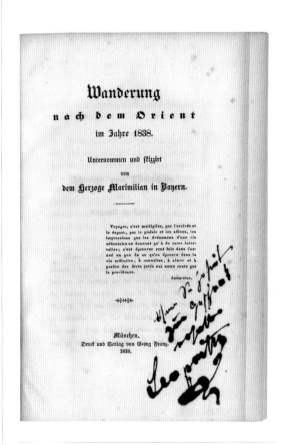

HERZOG MAXIMILIAN IN BAYERN, *Wanderung nach dem Orient im Jahre 1838*, München 1839. Frontispiece. Eg. Arch. & Lib., Edel Collection

Facing page:
Description de l'Égypte ... Antiquités, II, pl. 37.
Eg. Arch. & Lib., Edel Collection

A. MARIETTE, *Album du musée de Boulaq photographié par M.M. Délié et Béchard*, Le Caire 1872. Cover. Eg. Arch. & Lib., Varille Collection

Facing page:
A. MARIETTE, *Album* ... cit., pl. 2.

Following pages:
H. Béchard, Scene from the temple of Sety I at Abydos. The King offers an image of Maat. Eg. Arch. & Lib., Varille Collection

H. Béchard, The temple of Kom Ombo. Eg. Arch. & Lib., Varille Collection

In 1846, William Fox Talbot invented the talbotype (or calotype), a process whereby it is possible to print hundreds of images from one negative on light-sensitive paper. With this new technique the exposure time is much shorter, from a few minutes to ten seconds and a much wider range of tones can be obtained than with the daguerreotype. The calotype also allowed photographers to perform a number of experiments during the development of the image in the dark room. As a result, prints of various kinds began to appear, showing the diversity of styles of each photographer. Talbot used his invention to reproduce an inscription of Sety I found at Qasr Ibrim, documented in the brochure *The Talbotype Applied to Hieroglyphics*, published in London in 1846. But the first great photographic expedition along the Valley of the Nile was that of Maxime Du Camp, who in 1849, accompanied by his assistant Luigi Sassetti and his friend Gustave Flaubert, undertook a trip to Egypt and the Near East on behalf of the Académie des Inscriptions et Belles-Lettres in Paris. Du Camp worked hard to document the monuments from every point of view, placing local people next to them to show the proportions and lend an exotic touch to his pictures. For this work, and following the publication of his pictures in *Égypte, Nubie, Palestine et Syrie*, the first important French edition of calotypes, this great photographer was awarded the Legion of Honour.

The first photographers operating in the Near East towards the middle of the nineteenth century were mainly European travelers who, once they owned a camera, tried to reproduce the things they saw on their travels in the best possible way. Some of them were very talented, like Ernest Benecke, who photographed places and monuments in Syria, Egypt, and Nubia in 1852. Another was Félix Teynard, active in Egypt in 1851-52 and again in 1869, and John B. Green, who, though attracted by Egypt above all for its archaeological treasures, also endeavored to capture the beauty of the Egyptian landscape.

The early archaeologists, too, understood the value of photography and they used it widely. Auguste Mariette, who considered it an essential means of documentation, asked Théodule Devéria in 1858 to accompany him to Egypt, where they photographed many sites and monuments. Later, Mariette also engaged professional photographers, among them Hippolyte Délié and Émile Béchard. The two photographers shared a photographic studio in Cairo from 1870, and in 1872 they produced the *Album du Musée de Boulaq*, a copy of which is preserved in the Egyptological Library of the University of Milan. Béchard distinguishes himself not only with his talent in depicting ancient and modern monuments, but also for the skill in discovering and creating genre scenes. Thanks to the care and, above all, to the high quality of his production, Béchard was awarded the Golden Medal at the Universal Exhibition in Paris in 1878.

Another significant figure was the German Egyptologist Émile Brugsch who was Mariette's assistant and later curator of the Cairo collection but also an excellent photographer. He photographed many of the objects kept in the Museum for publication in the first volumes of the *Catalogue Général*.

Photographic techniques improved rapidly and in the 1850s Frederick Scott Archer introduced a process that produced a negative image on a transparent glass plate covered with wet collodion, that is, a solution of gun cotton in alcohol or ether, mixed with silver nitrate. The negatives were printed on albumen paper, which is paper treated with egg white. The prints were much stronger and of better quality than

N.º 118 Abydos, Temple de Séti I. Portrait de Séti I.   H. Béchard.

N° 42. Temple d'Ombos (Haute Égypte)   H. Béchard

those produced with the earlier processes yet they maintained the same wide range of tone as the calotype. Photographers had to use very cumbersome equipment, including dark rooms, tripods, very fragile glass plates of various sizes, as well as jars of distilled water, and the various chemical elements used for developing. Since collodion tends to dry very rapidly in the heat, the negatives had to be developed almost immediately after the impression of the image. This meant that photographers had to travel around with all their developing equipment, setting up their dark rooms on a wagon or more often on a *dahabiya*, the boat used to cruise along the Nile to reach the sites to be photographed. Despite these drawbacks, it was now easier to make hundreds of copies of the same image. To all intents and purposes photography had become a business.

Among those working with the collodion process, the first to realize the economic potential of the sale of photographs of Egyptian monuments was Francis Frith (active 1856-98). On his return to England, after a sojourn in Egypt and the Near East, he published his pictures in *Egypt and Palestine Photographed and Described*, issued in an edition of two thousand copies. In 1860 he established *F. Frith & Co.*, which sold a great number of images of various shapes and sizes and remained the largest printing house for photographs in Europe until the end of the nineteenth century.

Some particularly fine pictures by another English artist, Francis Bedford, who started to practice photography in 1853, can be found at the University of Milan, on deposit from a private collector. They were taken in Egypt in 1862, when Bedford was chosen by Queen Victoria to accompany the Prince of Wales, the future Edward VII, on his Tour of the East. Bedford took 172 photographs, which were shown at the London International Exhibition in the same year and which won him the Silver Medal at the Universal Exhibition in Paris in 1867.

A photographer named Meissner was also active during the 1860s. Little is known about him apart from the fact that he produced large-size photographs (406 x 260 mm) for commercial purposes in Egypt and Palestine. The Milanese Egyptological Archives have recently received on deposit a very rare photograph by him showing Pompey's Column in Alexandria.

One of the characteristics of photography in this period was the obvious influence of the traveler-painters who inspired both views and compositions. One photographer producing work of a high artistic quality was Gabriel Lekegian, and several of his pictures are in the Milanese Egyptological Archives. Not much is known about him, although he was a member of a large group of Armenian photographers active in Cairo and other cities in the Mediterranean and the Near East, and the prints that he developed and sold at the studio he opened in Shepheard's Hotel in Cairo were well-known. Lekegian also won a prize in the "Professional Artistic Photography" section at the Universal Exhibition in 1892. At first, his visiting cards mentioned Vienna, where he probably had contacts. Later he is listed among the photographers to the British Army of Occupation in Africa, probably during Kitchener's campaign in 1898. At the beginning of the twentieth century his prints bear the name *Lekegian & Co*, and are labelled *Photographie artistique*, in other words, they were presented to tourists, collectors, and artists as true works of art. Painters like Ludwig Deutsch and Enrico Tarenghi actually used some of Lekegians's photographs to enhance the background of some of their own compositions.

Facing page:
G. Lekegian, The Obelisk of Senuseret I at Heliopolis.
Eg. Arch. & Lib., Varille Collection

Following pages:
F. Bonfils, The Colossi of Memnon.
Eg. Arch. & Lib.

P. Dittrich, The Valley of the Kings.
Eg. Arch. & Lib.

J.P. Sebah, The Pyramids of Giza.
Eg. Arch. & Lib., Private Collection (long term deposit)

Obélisque d'Héliopolis (Matarieh) N° 21

Bonfils   Thèbes Colosses de Memnon (Égy

1027. THEBES TOMBEAUX des ROIS   P. DITTRICH

Pyramides de Gizeh (vue générale) 266   J.P. Sebah

In the second half of the nineteenth century, many photographers used to follow the route of wealthy travelers in Egypt where, with their pictures, they documented the landscapes, people, and monuments that attracted so much interest among westerners. Many of them opened studios in Egypt in the places most visited by tourists, especially in Cairo near the main hotels, but also in Alexandria and Luxor. Here they used to sell souvenirs and photos and sometimes they would also collaborate with archaeologists. In the Egyptological Archives of the University of Milan there are hundreds of images from this period, signed by the most famous photographers of the day, such as Bonfils, Dittrich, and Sebah.

The Frenchman Félix Bonfils was the first of a family of photographers and with his wife he opened a studio in Beirut in 1867. He also worked extensively in Egypt and, despite some initial problems, he soon succeeded in setting up a thriving business which spanned several decades. However, the early photographs signed by Bonfils may not have been taken by him; it seems that at the start he purchased some large-size photos from Tancrède Dumas because he did not possess a camera suitable for this type of shot. On his death in 1885, the *Maison Bonfils* passed to his wife and son who ran it until at least 1916 when Félix's assistant, Abraham Guiragossian, took over the business and kept it going until 1939. The Bonfils studio was extremely prolific, producing at least twenty-five thousand photos of Egypt and other countries in the Near East.

The German photographer P. Dittrich settled in Cairo in 1880 and in 1885. He joined the *Heymann, Laroche & Co.* of Cairo, which also had a studio in Constantinople, where Pascal Sebah made his debut. Sebah had been in Egypt since before 1878, and in collaboration with Antoine Laroche he photographed temples and ancient monuments and also produced an important collection of ethnographic pictures. After his death in 1886, his son Jean continued to run the studio successfully and *Foto Sebah* remained in business until 1952. He was certainly one of the most important photographers of the nineteenth century. His views and his genre photos of Athens, the Near East, and above all of Egypt and Nubia were very famous and he was awarded the silver medal at the Paris Universal Exhibition in 1878. Pascal Sebah is also mentioned in the famous *Baedeker guide* of 1885. The Egyptological Archives of the University of Milan has an exceptional collection of over seven hundred photographs by Sebah, which were bought privately in the antiquarian market and are now on long term deposit at the University.

Many photographic studios were also opened at Port Said where the influx of visitors increased significantly with the opening of the Suez Canal in 1869. The Greek photographer Peridis, for whom we have no biographical information, opened a studio in the city, where he worked with another Greek, Georgiladakis. Their photographs, signed *Peridis & Georgiladakis* or *Peridis & Co.*, were produced between 1870 and 1890.

Another photographer based in Port Said, in the very central Place de Consuls, was Hyppolite Arnoux, active in Egypt 1860-90. Often working on a boat, where he lived and had his dark room, Arnoux signed many photos of the excavations and other activities connected with the building of the Suez Canal. These images, originally intended for tourists, provide the most important documentation about the canal. They were also used by La Compagnie du Canal de Suez as its own

851 Esneh temple (intérieur)

J. P. Sebah

H Arnoux   Rade de Port Saïd

Caire — L'Entrée de la grande Pyramide.   237 — L. Fiorillo, Phot.

advertisement for the Paris Universal Exhibition of 1889.

From 1867 Arnoux also had a studio in Alexandria and for a time he worked with the brothers Constantin and Georges Zangaki, natives of the island of Milos, who settled in Port Said in the mid-1880s. The Zangaki brothers also worked in Cairo, producing not only many pictures of monuments and archaeological sites, but also ethnographic scenes, which satisfied the curiosity of tourists while, at same time, did not hurt local pride. These were posed photographs in which very careful attention was paid to scenographic features and details.

Meanwhile, photographic techniques were evolving rapidly and the mid-1870s saw the introduction of the gelatin dry plate to create a negative. This new product finally freed the photographer from the jars of water and chemical elements that until then had been part of his equipment. It was no longer necessary to cover each plate in order to maintain the image, and the negative could be stored for longer before developing. In 1885, the dry plates completely replaced the collodion wet plates, making the photographer's task much easier.

A curious variant in the photography of this period was linked to the invention of stereoscopy, which spread significantly between 1850 and 1890 and was widely used in Egypt. Stereoscopic vision allows us to see two images captured from two slightly different angles, separated by a distance similar to that between the eyes, thus obtaining a three-dimensional view of the scene. Thanks to this effect, even the most exotic locations became more realistic and more attractive.

One of the Italian photographers who settled in the country at this time was Luigi Fiorillo, a number of whose prints are kept in the Egyptological Archives of the University of Milan. In 1870 he settled in Alexandria, where he was active until at least 1898, producing mainly scenes from everyday life. For a time, Fiorillo was the official photographer of Prince Mohamed Toussoun Pasha. After showing his photographs in Naples in 1871 and at the Paris Universal Exhibition of 1878, he started to collaborate, in 1880, with another photographer, as confirmed by some prints signed *Marquis & Fiorillo*, which depict views of Jerusalem and Algeria and include some rare pictures of Mecca. They are dated up until the beginning of the twentieth century.

Another well-known photographer was Antonio Beato, whose production covers the period from 1860 to 1900. The numerous photographs by Beato belonging to the University of Milan were shown at an exhibition in Bologna in 2008, which then transferred to the Mubarak Library in Luxor in 2009. Some of them were also published in the accompanying catalogue. Between 1868 and 1869 Beato had a small studio at the Shepheard's Hotel in Cairo. During this period he used a logo which bore his name and the print of a pyramid between two sphinxes. At the bottom it says *Photographie Antoine Beato, rue de Muski Caire (Egypte)*. From 1862, however, his main studio was in Luxor, where there was less competition, but many sites to photograph, some in the Theban area and others where the Nubian temples built by the pharaohs stand, further away but more easily accessible than from Cairo. In the Theban tombs, Beato was one of the first to experiment with illumination by means of a special lamp, invented in 1880, which burnt magnesium and therefore did not blacken the walls. Other photographers on the contrary continued to use torches and candles which, with the help of mirrors, illuminated the wall they wanted to photograph. This old technique, however, damaged the walls, blackening them with smoke.

A. Beato, Tomb of Nakht at Sheikh 'Abd el-Qurna (TT 52).
Eg. Arch. & Lib.

Facing page:
L. Fiorillo, Tourists climbing the Great Pyramid at Giza.
Eg. Arch. & Lib.

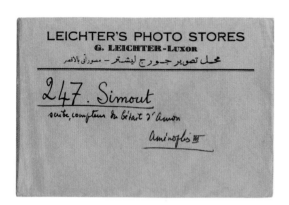

LEICHTER'S PHOTO STORES
G. LEICHTER-LUXOR
محل تصوير جـورج ليشـتر – مصورﭐي بالاقصر

247. Simout
scribe, compteur du trésor d'Amon
Aminophis III

Leichter's Photo Stores. Envelope with notes
by A. Varille.
Eg. Arch. & Lib., Varille Collection

Agfa Photo G. Leichter Luxor. Envelope
from the Leichter studio.
Eg. Arch. & Lib., Varille Collection

Facing page:
A. Beato, The Temple of Luxor and the house
where Beato initially lived, viewed from the Nile.
Eg. Arch. & Lib.

Although photographs of Antonio Beato himself have never been found, some of his pictures show the exact place where his studio and his home used to stand. Initially he lived in a house just in front of the Temple of Luxor, but somewhere between 1870 and 1880 he moved to the Luxor Hotel, behind the temple. Here he remained until his death in 1905.

Two of the Egyptologists who closely followed the work of these photographers, especially Beato, were Georges Legrain and Gaston Maspero. The latter was the Director of the Egyptian Antiquities Service from 1881 to 1886 and from 1899 to 1914. He immediately recognized the importance of the work of photographers in Egypt and the function of photography as a means of documentation. He met Antonio Beato in Luxor several times, bought his pictures, and often mentioned him in letters to his wife. Following Legrain's advice, he managed to purchase some of Beato's archaeological plates and a number of prints depicting archaeological subjects for the Cairo Museum in 1907. In 1911, Maspero also used many of Beato's photographs to illustrate the volume he edited on Egypt in the series *Histoire générale de l'art*, while other photos were used by Legrain for his work *Les temples de Karnak*, published posthumously in 1929.

After Beato's death, his wife put over 1,500 of his plates up for sale and about 200 of these are still in the Photographic Archive in Cairo Museum, signed by him or attributed to him with a fair degree of certainty. In October 2008, during the exhibition *The History of the Egyptian Museum*, organized at the Egyptian Museum in Cairo by the Director of the museum itself and the Chair of Egyptology of the University of Milan, some of these plates were exhibited, still in the original wooden boxes made at the beginning of the twentieth century when they arrived at the museum.

Towards the end of the nineteenth century the German architect Max Junghaendel was active in Egypt as a photographer. He is best known for his illustrations for the work by Georg Ebers, *Aegypten: Heliogravuren nach Original-Aufnahmen mit Vorwort and erlaüterndem Text* (1893), and for being a pioneer of artistic photo-engraving. Junghaendel produced just a very few views of Egypt printed on silk and one of these rare specimens, which appeared on the antiquarian market in 2010, was purchased by a Milanese patron and deposited in the University's Egyptological Archives.

The Archives also house many documents of Félix Guilmant, who was a friend and relative of Victor Loret. Guilmant was active in Egypt as a designer and photographer in the late nineteenth and early twentieth century. He was among the first to use photography as a means of complete epigraphic documentation of a tomb. From his photographs he produced very precise facsimiles of texts and scenes, using a method that was later widely adopted by Egyptologists.

From 1910, a photographer originally from Bolzano, Heinz Leichter, was operating in Luxor. He opened a shop not far away from Antonio Beato's studio and worked for both tourists and for the Oriental Institute in Chicago. Alexandre Varille also used that studio and shop for the purchase of equipment and the development of his photographs, as evidenced by the numerous envelopes, photographs, and postcards with Leichter's name preserved in the Milan Archives. Some envelopes also bear the label *Leichter's Photo Store. Georges Leichter. Editor Artist & Photographer. Luxor (Upper Egypt)*. Georges, Heinz's son and collaborator, sold the business after his father's death in 1940 to

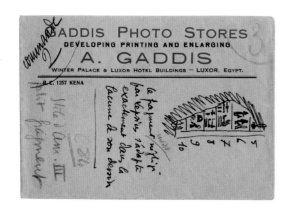

Gaddis Photo Stores. Envelope with notes
by A. Varille.
Eg. Arch. & Lib., Varille Collection

H. Nassibian. Envelope.
Eg. Arch. & Lib., Varille Collection

Facing page:
H. Leichter, The Great Temple of Karnak.
Eg. Arch. & Lib., Varille Collection

Following pages:
Morès, *Au Grand Temple de Karnak, 1ᵉʳ Janvier 1927.*
The arrival of King Fuad I at the Great Temple
of Karnak.
Eg. Arch. & Lib., Private Collection (long term deposit)

Morès, *Au Grand Temple de Karnak, 1ᵉʳ Janvier 1927.*
King Fuad I visiting the Great Temple of Karnak
with P. Lacau.
Eg. Arch. & Lib., Private Collection (long term deposit)

Morès, *Au Grand Temple de Karnak, 1ᵉʳ Janvier 1927.*
The first court and the Hypostyle Hall
of the Great Temple of Karnak.
Eg. Arch. & Lib., Private Collection (long term deposit)

Hassan Ahmed El Adly. The latter worked mainly as a laboratory photographer, but continued to print Leichter's clichés. Many renowned Egyptologists used Adly's shop. Besides Varille, Clément Robichon and Jean Leclant, for example, were also regular customers.

Attaya Gaddis too, Beato's young assistant, who in 1907 started the photographic business that would last right through to the 1970s, seems to have used some of Beato's plates at the beginning of his career when he inherited the business in Luxor. Gaddis opened a souvenir shop at the Winter Palace and for almost twenty years, from 1912 to 1930, he collaborated with Georges Seif, who became a photographer in Luxor after having worked for the Egyptian Railways. Their names, in the form *Phot. A. Gaddis & G. Seif Louqsor,* often appear stamped on the back of photographic prints, many of which are preserved in the Archives of the University of Milan. The negative plates, however, do not bear any signature. Indeed, from the late nineteenth century, it became increasingly rare to sign photographs and after 1910 the practice was dropped completely. Thus the idea of the photograph as a work of art or a "photographic painting" gradually disappeared. Photography was rapidly becoming industrialized as its popularity spread. Some photographic publishers even used the best-known prints of famous nineteenth-century artist-photographers. One of these was *Schroeder-Cie Zurich,* who added his own name or the brand name *Photoglob* to the prints, which were often by Bonfils. Many of the images marked in this way are documented in the collection of Varille, who may have bought them at Gaddis's shop. It was here that the French archaeologist used to purchase photographs and have his own developed, as we know from the numerous envelopes and the photographs kept in his archives. In this shop, Gaddis's heirs still sell picture postcards of their ancestor's plates, some of which were probably the work of Antonio Beato.

Varille used to live for part of the year in Luxor and at other times in Cairo. When he was in the capital, he used different laboratories to develop his photographs, including the Kodak laboratory and that of H. Nassibian. There are thousands of pictures in Varille's archives, mostly taken by himself. He was passionate about photography and he understood the fundamental importance of this medium for documenting sites, monuments, objects, and all the stages of the excavations. His extraordinary collection also contains around four hundred photographs of sites in Morocco, Algeria, Tunisia, Libya, Lebanon, Syria, and Palestine.

As we have seen, the Egyptological Archives of the University of Milan are home to hundreds of photographs and plates by the nineteeth century's most famous protagonists in this new field, as well as thousands of twentieth-century photographs, including prints, plates, and negatives. They feature archaeological sites and monuments from all over Egypt, Egyptian and Nubian landscapes, and genre scenes typical of the turn of the century. They also show the phases of excavations and the objects found in Egyptian museums all over the world. The gathering began with the Edel Collection in 1999 and has been steadily enriched, mainly due to the Varille Collection (which includes those of Loret and Quibell, with about two thousand photographs) and the Bothmer Collection.

Purchases on the antiquarian market have also continued on a fairly regular basis over the past ten years. Among these is a splendid album, dating from around 1880, which includes sixty albumen prints (measuring about 210 x 260 mm) mounted on sheets of cardboard,

signed by Arnoux, Beato, and Fiorillo, and two other albums containing rare photographs of Nubia taken by Beato. Early in 2008, an important series of old photos was added to the collection, thanks to a generous gift made by Ars Libri, ltd., Boston.

Another album, produced by Morès, *Photographe de SM le Roi*, Alexandrie, deposited in the Archives in Milan by a private collector, contains forty-one photographs, measuring approximately 112 x 167 mm and bearing the embossed stamp of the author. These were taken at the Temple of Karnak on January 1, 1927, as stated on the first page of the album, during the visit of King Fuad I. The King was welcomed and then accompanied on his visit by Pierre Lacau, then the Director of the Egyptian Antiquities Service. On the same occasion he also visited the Temple of Luxor and the main monuments of the Theban West Bank. Other versions of the same scenes depicting Fuad I with Lacau as his guide are also in the Lacau Collection of the University of Milan.

Another extraordinary album that used to belong to Alexandre Varille has been deposited in the Milanese Archives by a private collector. It contains twenty-one aerial photographs, signed in the negative *Kofler, Cairo, 1914*. This album is particularly important because it is probably the first organic collection of aerial photographs of ancient monuments taken for documentary rather than artistic purposes. Two of Kofler's photos were used in the English guide to Luxor for the sick entitled *Luxor as a Health Resort*. The second edition was published by Drs Dunn and Worthington, who added the two aerial photos to show the beauty of the place – a complete novelty at the time. Moreover, until a few years ago, Kofler, who took the pictures, was unknown in the history of photography, despite his considerable technical skills. Following extensive research, which is still ongoing, a link has emerged between him and Heinz Leichter. They had probably already met in Egypt when they were both interned in the Saint Clement internment camp in Malta in 1915, as proved by some photographs in the Leichter Collection. The two groups of photos bear the same signature in an identical handwriting. On the photos taken in Malta one can read *Kofler, 1915* and *Kofler Malta, Malta-Cairo 1916*. As already mentioned, Varille used Leichter's studio in Luxor, and this is where he may have come across Kofler's album.

However, Kofler and his collection must already have been well known at least in Egypt in the 1920s and 1930s, because five of his pictures were published by Capart in *Thèbes : la gloire d'un grand passé*, in 1925. Another four pictures by Kofler were used by Capart himself in his *Propos sur l'art égyptien*, in 1931. One more was published in the work that Varille wrote with Clément Robichon, *Le temple du scribe royal Amenhotep fils de Hapou*, published in 1936; yet another can be found in Paul Barguet's volume of 1962, *Le temple d'Amon-Rê à Karnak : essai d'exégèse*. Two more photographs by Kofler, belonging to Georges Daressy are kept in the Archives of the Collège de France in Paris.

After Kofler's excellent pioneering work, aerial photography for documentary and archaeological purposes spread rapidly in Egypt. One of those who used it was James Henry Breasted, who made his first flight to take photographs of the Memphite necropolis on 13 January 1920, on a Royal Air Force plane. Breasted wrote in his diary:

The Royal Air Force has shown me hundreds and hundreds of air views of Egypt, Palestine and Syria, but practically nothing of use to us archaeologists.

Kofler, *Photographies des Pyramides et de Louxor prises en aeroplane par Kofler, Cairo*. Cover.
Eg. Arch. & Lib., Varille Collection

Facing page:
Kofler, The Temple of Luxor, in *Photographies* ... cit.
Eg. Arch. & Lib., Varille Collection

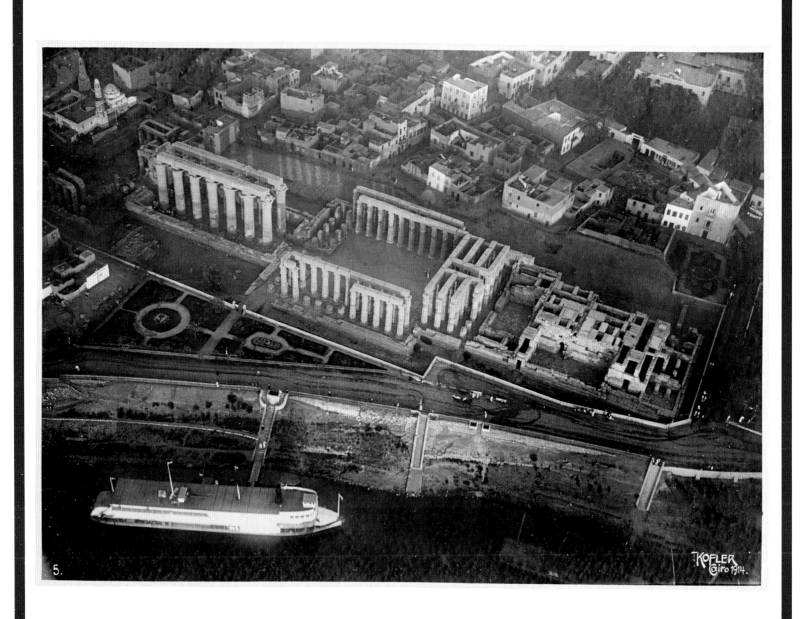

5.

The Air Commodore gave orders to his flyers to make special photographs for us of the whole margin of the Desert from Gizeh to Dahshur; but I wanted to take some of my own.

(C. BREASTED, *Pioneer to the Past*, Chicago 1943, pp. 258-259)

In the 1940s the French archaeologist Alexandre Varille acquired a certain number of aerial photographs taken by the Royal Air Force, among them some views of the Theban West Bank as well as the islands of Philae and Sehel. These are now in the Archives of Egyptology of the University of Milan. These have recently been enriched by the extraordinary photographic collection of Bernard V. Bothmer: over ten thousand photographs, mainly of statues and other objects kept in public and private collections all over the world. For most of them frontal, lateral, and posterior views were systematically taken and used whenever possible to reconstruct or connect pieces kept in different collections as well as for art historical purposes.

Thus, photography evolved into a working tool for Egyptologists in both fields, excavations and library research.

Egypt in Modern Culture

Aspects of Ancient Egypt in Nineteenth Century Painting

Fernando Mazzocca

III. *Aspects of Ancient Egypt in Nineteenth Century Painting*

Fernando Mazzocca

On view at the Galleria Nazionale d'Arte Moderna in Rome is a large and impressive painting by Federico Faruffini entitled *Il sacrificio egiziano di una vergine al Nilo*. It represents an episode in historical painting in nineteenth century Italy, where themes inspired by historical events and the art of ancient Egypt were relatively uncommon. It is also unique because of the rarity of the theme depicted, and the originality of its bold formality. The scene has an almost musical rhythm, as if the artist wanted to transpose the particular cadences of Egyptian painting into a modern key, where the notes are represented by vibrant colors, enhanced by the painting's long, narrow format. These features could explain the lukewarm response when the painting was shown in an exhibition at the Accademia delle Belle Arti di Brera (Milan 1865). The scene depicted required a detailed description in the exhibition catalog, explaining that:

It was an Egyptian custom to sacrifice once a year a virgin to the Nile, the river which made their fields fertile, thus placating the spirit of evil with a human life. The artist has attempted to reconstruct the funeral ceremony, with the inclusion of such features as the Egyptian rites of lustral water, sacred music, the passions of the multitude and the pain of the victim's relatives and her beloved, who throws himself into the river when her body rises to the surface.

Confronted with such a disturbing representation of the cruel yet fascinating customs of that ancient civilization, even the most benevolent critics reacted negatively, although acknowledging the painter's genius in what were defined as "aberrations." In the light of such hostility, apparently shared by a public that could not appreciate the novelty of the work or the decadent mentality of the artist, Faruffini moved to Paris, where the reception was completely different. After receiving a medal at the *Salon* in 1866, he presented the painting, which had aroused such controversy in Italy, again at the *Salon* the following year. This time it was a success, enhanced by engravings of the painting by the artist himself, reproduced by Cadart in two editions.

While the many preliminary drawings reveal the work's long and complex gestation, there is no evidence to explain why the artist chose such an unusual subject, found in literature but seldom in painting. One possibility is that the theme was inspired by the works of the Anglo-Dutch painter Sir Lawrence Alma-Tadema, the best known of the historical painters engaged in producing scenes from ancient Egyptian life. However, both the style and the imaginative interpretation of the visual sources are extremely personal as can be seen from one of the preliminary sketches, which refers back to the first volume of plates of *Antiquités* in the *Description de l'Égypte*, or the *Île de Philae* by André Dutertre. The figures on the extreme left, the two figures on the extreme right, and the kneeling servants are taken from the reliefs of the Temple of Philae.

Facing page:
Federico Faruffini, *Il sacrificio egiziano di una vergine al Nilo*, 1865.
Rome, Galleria Nazionale d'Arte Moderna
(courtesy of Ministero per i Beni e le Attività Culturali)

Faruffini's painting, which was intended to be understood in an international context such as the Paris *Salon*, appeared at a time when Egypt was a popular theme in nineteenth century historical painting. The new knowledge acquired of that ancient civilization, thanks to Napoleon's campaign, the subsequent archaeological expeditions and the constant transfer of works of art to European museums, marked a turning point in Egyptomania, which also affected painting. Whereas previous references to Egypt had been rather generic, during the nineteenth century painters became increasingly careful to appear credible. They consulted the latest publications, drew inspiration from the most recent archaeological discoveries, or turned directly to the experts, who willingly offered their help. Citing archaeological sources not only served as a guarantee for the artists themselves but it became a way of involving the public, which was becoming more and more fascinated by that still mysterious civilization, thanks to sensational discoveries and the creation of new museums.

A monumental painting entitled *I membri della spedizione franco-toscana in Egitto presso le rovine di Tebe* by Giuseppe Angelelli, now in the Museo Archeologico in Florence, is a sensational display of Europe's fascination with Egypt and the relationship between artists and the great explorer-archaeologists, much loved by the public. The expedition was sponsored by the Granduca di Toscana and by France, and the painter himself took part in it. He was engaged as an illustrator by Ippolito Rosellini, head of the mission along with Jean-François Champollion. Angelelli's drawings form the basis of the impressive illustrated volume by Rosellini, *I monumenti dell'Egitto e della Nubia*, published between 1832 and 1834. The painting was commissioned by the Granduca, and while the ever-dissatisfied artist started it in 1829, he only completed it in 1836 after considerable effort. It shows a large group scene in which the members of the expedition are positioned hierarchically. Champollion is seated in the centre, with Rosellini and his uncle the architect Gaetano behind him. The Sheikh Awad, with his back to the viewer, closes the composition on the right. In the foreground toward the left, the figure of the French painter Alexandre Adolphe Duchesne stands out. He reclines in a languid, romantic pose with one hand resting on a small picture and his open box of watercolors beside him. Eight other members of the expedition, including Angelelli himself, are grouped together in conversation on the left, but the most interesting feature of the painting is the faithful representation of the majestic ruins of Thebes and the desert in the background, dominated by a flaming sky and dotted with palm trees, stretching into the horizon.

In this fascinating picture, which aroused the enthusiasm of the German archaeologist, Richard Lepsius who corresponded with Rosellini, the image of the ancient lost civilization is represented by the presence of Theban architectural features, including an obelisk, which are reproduced clearly and accurately. This architecture became a characteristic element of biblical historical painting set in Egypt, painted mainly in the first half of the century.

A significant example of this trend is *La morte dei primogeniti d'Egitto*, a large canvas stored in the Pinacoteca di Brera. The Marquis Filippo Villani of Milan, a collector and art critic, commissioned in 1838 a painter from Belluno, Pietro Paoletti, to paint the picture that was presented at the Accademia di Brera exhibition in 1840. This tragic episode was the occasion for a grandiose choral narration, described as follows by Tullio Dandolo:

[...] il tumulto tremendo della reggia egiziana par che si prolunghi e si confonda con quel dei fuggenti fin dove lo sguardo può scernere in un lume incerto di luna che viene sfumando in quel dell'aurora nascente.

The costumes and the impressive architectural setting, praiseworthy for its archaeological accuracy, dominate the complex narrative, which recalls other paintings inspired by the captivity of the Hebrews in Egypt and their liberation. The English painter Benjamin Haydon led in this particular area of historical painting in the 1820s; his sources included the *Description de l'Égypte* and the volumes illustrated by Dominique Vivant Denon. He was in direct contact with Belzoni, and, as he records in his *Journal*, he studied the Egyptian antiquities housed in the Louvre, producing a series of pictures with a biblical-Egyptian theme based on the documentation he would have seen. Thus painters moved from representing historical events in a generic setting toward a more faithful reconstruction showing the gigantic proportions of that ancient architecture, which – in the case of skillful illustrators like John Martin, David Roberts, Gustave Doré, and Edward-John Poynter – gave rise to a new dreamlike or scenographic dimension.

For the large canvas, *The Seventh Plague of Egypt* (Museum of Fine Arts, Boston), Martin, who was the first curator of the John Soane Museum in London and one of the protagonists of Egyptomania, used texts by the ancient Greek historians Strabo, Herodotus, and Diodorus, along with the most up-to-date illustrated material. However, he interpreted his sources with such visionary power that the sequence of those colossal architectural structures were projected into a unreal sense of space and time, overwhelmed by the elements of nature. In Roberts's *Departure of the Israelites*, the flight of imagination, inspired by the poetics of the sublime and the ominous atmosphere created by Martin, assumes a richer language determined by a more attentive observation of Denon's work. The huge dimensions of the architecture appear to be even more accentuated, carefully observed from the real thing, even though nothing of this size had ever been realized in Egypt on such an impressive scale. The striking feature is the expansion of space, its perspective spreads out into infinity: vertiginous, labyrinthine sequences of columns follow one after another leading to a sea of pyramids that fade away towards the horizon. This particular solution can be attributed to the artist's previous experience in London and Edinburgh in theatrical scenography, where Egyptian elements were widely used. The impressive scenic power of this picture seems to herald the more ambitious solutions used in the popular Hollywood blockbusters, in particular the unforgettable movies of Cecil B. DeMille.

While for the English we talk of scenographic painters, for the French it is more appropriate to use the term painter-archaeologists. The latter succeeded in reproducing a more reliable image of those ancient events, such as a more realistic geographical environment thanks to a more precise study of the written and visual sources. In addition to visiting museums and consulting documentation more assiduously, they had direct contact with experts who had actually been to Egypt. This was the case for painters working at the Accademia di Francia in Rome, including the Lyonese Victor Orsel, a great interpreter of biblical themes. These painters, along with Paoletti who shared their experiences, directly consulted Champollion, who was a major influence.

One of the exemplary protagonists of this trend is Adrien

Guignet. His masterpiece *Cambyse et Psamménite* (Musée du Louvre, Paris) was successfully presented at the *Salon* in 1841. The French writer Théophile Gautier described it in 1869, when the seductive paintings of Alma-Tadema had overshadowed the works of the old archaeological painters, as:

[...] une œuvre des plus remarquables, où la recerche archéologique ne nuit en rien au mouvement, à l'effet et à l'originalité.

This originality is due to featuring not only the monuments, such as the ever-present pyramid, but also to including costumes, animals (two enormous elephants), ornaments, and creating an atmosphere similar to that typically found in Orientalist painting. In this case archaeological reliability merges with "imagination," defined again by Gautier as "un des grands mérites" of the painter who has "le don très rare de rêver un site, une époque, un effet, de les voir avec l'œil de l'esprit et les rendre comme s'ils posaient réellement devant lui."

Meanwhile, thanks mainly to the influence of novelists, biblical themes were increasingly being replaced by historical themes that recalled the mysterious and exotic rituals of ancient Egyptian life. The *Roman de la momie* (1858) by Gautier, and the *Ägyptische Königstochter* (1864) by the famous German Egyptologist and novelist Georg Moritz Ebers were two international bestsellers, which inspired generations of painters and illustrators, and ultimately influenced the cinema of the following century. In historical paintings of the second half of the nineteenth century, scenes of everyday life, set in antiquity and sometimes involving Egypt, became more and more common. They were theatrical paintings in which painters displayed a variety of skills as portrait painters, costumers, scenographers, decorators, and always showed they were particularly attentive to accessories and scrupulous over details.

For example Alma-Tadema, who dominated the field, would consult fundamental texts such as *The Manners and Customs of the Ancient Egyptians* (1837) by Sir John Gardner Wilkinson, or the *Histoire de l'Art Égyptien, d'après les monuments, depuis les temps les plus reculés jusqu'à la domination romaine* by Prisse d'Avennes, written 1858-1877. He also copied exhibits on display at the British Museum. It was Ebers who had fueled Alma-Tadema's passion for ancient Egypt and taught him to become familiar with the customs and mentality of the people. Between 1854 and 1904, twenty-six of Alma-Tadema's paintings had an Egyptian theme, making him the most prolific and significant painter of the genre.

His masterpiece, *An Egyptian Widow*, in the Rijksmuseum in Amsterdam, shows the extent to which he was able to render more persuasively than anyone else the fascination and mystery of that lost world, whose images he interspersed with those of ancient Greece and Rome. In this moderately sized picture, painted in 1872, he represents with extraordinary care and illusionary skill the interior of a temple, of which every detail is faithfully reconstructed. The architectural decorations, murals, furnishings, and the absolute fidelity with which all the archaeological details are reproduced create an effect of great authenticity, as if the sad rite were being performed today before our very eyes. At the same time, the background behind the columns, showing a sphinx and a statue surrounded by a profusion of elegant green plants, recalls the Egyptian Court at Crystal Palace for the Universal Ex-

hibition in London in 1851. But it was the precise reproduction of a mummy, the support and stela from the British Museum, and a harp preserved in the Louvre that guaranteed the archaeological authenticity of his work to a public who, having visited the museums, demanded historical fidelity. It was only in 1902 that Alma-Tadema was able to fulfil his dream of visiting Egypt, on the occasion of the inauguration of the first Aswan dam. On his return he painted one of his most famous pictures, *The Finding of Moses*, which, like all his paintings, was to make a strong impression on cinematography in the first half of the twentieth century.

While the Anglo-Dutch painters alternated Egyptian themes with those inspired by ancient Greece and Rome, others, such as Jules-Jean-Antoine Lecomte du Noüy tended more towards Orientalism. Inspired by Gautier's *Roman de la momie*, Lecomte du Noüy painted *Les porteurs de mauvaises nouvelles* (1872), *Ramsès dans son harem* (1885-86), *La tristesse du pharaon* (1901), all of which captured the popular imagination. Meanwhile, in the decadent Vienna of the Hapsburgs, the great academic Hans Makart, the undisputed leader in the field of official historical painting, introduced a heavy dose of eroticism along with Egyptian customs in his monumental painting *Die Niljagd der Kleopatra* (1876). The legendary life and death of Cleopatra along with biblical themes were favorite subjects with painters. In the sixteenth and seventeenth centuries, Shakespeare's play had already made the unfortunate queen one of the most popular heroines among artists.

Even though new studies had restored Cleopatra to her rightful historical place, that is, in the Hellenistic Period, the painters of the second half of the nineteenth century identified her with the myth of the *femme fatale*. The artists projected her into the fictional environment of the Egypt of the pharaohs, which was quite far from her, or, with an even more evident distortion of reality, into a medieval oriental setting inspired by *The Arabian Nights*. Cleopatra became the protagonist, for example, in the works of Austrian painter Hans Makart and French painter Jean-Léon Gérôme, in spectacular pictures where the exotic components were extremely suggestive, evoking the mysterious splendors of a lost antiquity. Inserting her in extremely unlikely episodes, the artists spread before Cleopatra all the riches of the Orient and of Africa: gold, pearls, damask, silk, ivory, ebony, incense, ostrich feathers, leopards skins, and even tigers. A great painting of 1887, *Cléopatre essayant des poisons sur des condamnés à mort* (Musée Royal des Beaux-Arts, Antwerp) by one of the principal pompier painters, Alexandre Cabanel, introduces an episode that is totally unrelated to the historical reality of the cruel woman, evoked through an atmosphere laden with tension and eroticism. The anachronistic evocation of the Temple of Philae mixes with physiognomies and customs inspired by what is seductive and exotic, which are completely mannered and confected.

Facing page:
Alexandre Cabanel, *Cléopatre essayant des poisons sur des condamnés à mort*, 1887.
Antwerp, Musée Royal des Beaux-Arts

Following page:
Detail of Alexandre Cabanel, *Cléopatre essayant ...* cit., that inspired the image on the early twentieth century cigarette box *O'San*.

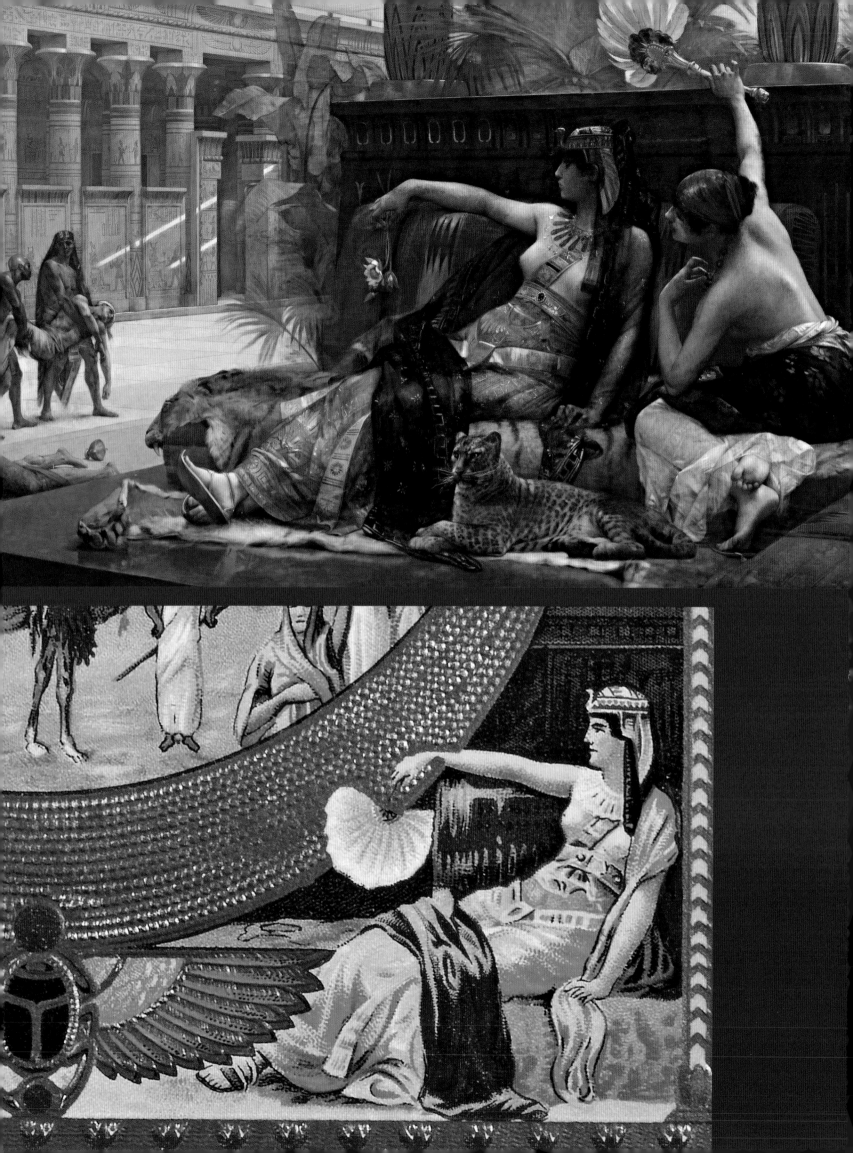

Walls and Dishes
Gaetano Lodi, an Italian Painter for the Khedive Ismail Pasha

Patrizia Piacentini

(Ed.ni Brogi) 4608. MILANO Ottagono della Galleria Vittorio Emanuele.

IV. *Walls and Dishes*

Gaetano Lodi, an Italian Painter for the Khedive Ismail Pasha

Patrizia Piacentini

In 2004, a private collector offered the Chair of Egyptology of the University of Milan the opportunity to study and publish an extraordinary series of preparatory watercolors for the Egyptian-style porcelain State service of the Khedive Ismail Pasha. They are signed by Gaetano Lodi, whose important role in the "Egyptian revival" of the nineteenth century was almost unknown up until then, despite his wide knowledge and use of ancient Egyptian themes and decorative patterns.

Gaetano Lodi was born in Crevalcore (Bologna) on November 27, 1830. Although he came from a modest family, in 1853 he started to take classes in decoration at the Accademia di Belle Arti in Bologna, where he eventually was appointed Professore di Ornato (Professor of Ornamentation) in 1878. He became interested in artistic ceramics in his youth, working as an apprentice in the atelier of Giuseppe Manfredini. In Bologna, he met and also worked with Angelo Minghetti, who was one of the most prolific producers of decorated porcelain in the mid nineteenth century. With this firm, he created his first floreal decorations on dishware, marked by an "M" on the back.

After having been an apprentice in the atelier of his Professore di Ornato Giuseppe Badiali, in about 1856, he became an assistant to Andrea Pesci. With Pesci, he painted a variety of churches and palaces. For a short period, he also worked with Camillo Leoni to create the elements of the scenography used for the visit of Pope Pius IX to Bologna in 1857. Most notably, he decorated the triumphal arches provisionally erected in Castelfranco Emilia (Modena) and in Cento (Ferrara). He was paid for this work for the first time, marking the beginning of his professional artistic career. In 1859-60, Lodi and Andrea Pesci painted various buildings in Bologna – Palazzo Dal Monte, Palazzo Bonora, and Palazzo Rossi – as well as the ceiling of the theater in San Giovanni in Persiceto, near Bologna. This experience was the first of a series of collaborations or personal commissions to decorate theaters: the Eleonora Duse – former Teatro Brunetti – in Bologna, together with the painter Valentino Solmi, in 1864-65; the Opéra in Paris, with the painter Paul Baudry, in 1867; one theater in Livorno from when he received the commission in 1876 to 1877; and the one in his native town of Crevalcore from when he was commissioned in 1877 to 1881.

In 1862 after decorating the Sala delle Signore in the Caffè del Corso in Bologna, he started to decorate the porticoes of the Banca d'Italia, in the same city. The paintings of the twenty-five vaults, of which fifteen are on the piazza Cavour side and the rest on the via Farini side, were interrupted in 1863 when Lodi was called up for military duty. They were eventually completed in 1865. The decoration is based on a figurative neo-Renaissance and Rafaellesque style, rich in centaurs, racemes, garlands, grotesque masks, and birds, in which Pompeian red dominates. In order to glorify the recent unification of Italy, each vault was divided into four sections to represent different episodes of Italy's

Portrait of Gaetano Lodi painting. Photograph. Private Collection

Facing page:
Galleria Vittorio Emanuele II in Milan.
Photograph by G. Brogi, *c.* 1880
Firenze, Raccolte Musei Fratelli Alinari, Collezione Favrod

Following pages:
Wall of one room in the Giza Palace of Ismail Pasha.
Drawing by Gaetano Lodi.
Bologna, Istituzione Galleria d'Arte Moderna, Collezioni storiche

Ceiling of the Salone al pian terreno in the Giza Palace of Ismail Pasha.
Drawing by Gaetano Lodi.
Bologna, Istituzione Galleria d'Arte Moderna, Collezioni storiche

The Giza Palace, decorated by Gaetano Lodi.
Photograph by J.P. Sebah.
Eg. Arch. & Lib., Private Collection (long term deposit)

The Giza Palace, decorated by Gaetano Lodi.
Photograph by J.P. Sebah.
Eg. Arch. & Lib., Private Collection (long term deposit)

SALONE
di prima Pianta
dell' PALAZZO
di S.A.R. CHIVE
a BELLETO

197 Musée de Ghisel

ancient and modern history: its civilization, nature, explorations and geographic discoveries, and heraldic shields. It also included Bologna's history. In their time, Lodi's paintings were thought to be such a source of inspiration that the students from the Accademia di Belle Arti were sent to admire the porticoes and learn about art, history, and even morality.

In 1865, he also painted the interior of Palazzo Vacchi in Imola, near Bologna, and started the decoration with floreal motifs of the Stanza Ottagonale, now housing the library, in the Banca d'Italia in Florence. He also decorated the Villa Reale Medicea in Poggio a Caiano, near Florence, and the Reale Casino del Gombo in San Rossore. For the Savoia family, Lodi painted the imposing staircase of the Palazzo Reale in Turin, as well as the porticoes of the Palazzo di Città. Two years later he was appointed Pittore ornatista onorario della Real Casa.

At the beginning of 1867, he went to Paris, where he lived in rue St Dominique, in the seventh *arrondissement*. Paul Baudry invited Lodi to collaborate with him and his brother, Ambroise Baudry, on the neo-Renaissance style decoration of the Opéra's *grand foyer*, picturing the history of music. In August, he returned to Italy to help architect Giuseppe Mengoni decorate the Galleria Vittorio Emanuele II in Milan. In its central vault, four large allegorical mosaics represent Europe, America, Asia, and Africa, the latter personified by a lady looking like an Egyptian queen, and by a farmer with the typical trapezoidal pharaonic headdress, with an ancient Egyptian building in the background.

Between 1869 and 1871, Lodi was appointed Professore ordinario (Full Professor) and Professore corrispondente of the Accademia Fiorentina, and became Cavaliere della Corona d'Italia (Knight of the Crown of Italy) and Socio onorario of the Real Accademia Centrale in Bologna. Continuing his exceptional career, in the following year he painted the emblems of the main Italian municipalities in the Salone dei Corazzieri, Palazzo del Quirinale in Rome, to celebrate the unification of Italy.

But his greatest challenge had yet to come: in 1872 he decided to go to Egypt, as attested in a letter that he sent on July 28 to Luigi Vassalli, who was working in Egypt in the Egyptian Antiquities Service directed by Auguste Mariette. The Khedive Ismail Pasha, who ruled the country from 1863 to 1879, wanted his houses, palaces, furniture, and even daily objects to look like the most fashionable European ones. As a result, he invited and attracted famous western architects, artists, and craftsmen to Cairo. By 1865, the French firm Christofle had already supplied him with an astonishing six hundred-piece service; the cutlery was in the traditional Louis XVI pattern.

Gaetano Lodi, who had acquired a very good reputation as painter and designer in Italy and France, was called for two main reasons: first, to design an imposing porcelain State service in pharaonic style, and secondly, to decorate the harem and the *salamelech* in Ismail's Giza Palace, which would have housed the Egyptian collection in the last decade of the nineteenth century (see Chapter I). This palace was enlarged during the 1870s by Lodi's friend Ambroise Baudry, brother of Paul, with whom Gaetano had worked in Paris a few years before. In Egypt, Lodi developed his very personal, eclectic style, in which floreal, neo-Renaissance, and neo-Baroque motifs were mixed with Arab and ancient Egyptian motifs, resulting in a spectacular and particularly rich composition. For the decoration of the palace, Lodi was as-

Gaetano Lodi with his wife Maria Messeri and their sons Luigi Scipione and Cesare Francesco. Photograph. Private Collection

Facing page:
Gaetano Lodi, preparatory watercolor for the porcelain service of the Khedive Ismail Pasha, 1872-1874. Private Collection

Chandelier. Watercolor by Gaetano Lodi.
Private Collection

Chandelier. Drawing, in L.G. FIGUIER, *Le meraviglie dell'industria. Il vetro e le porcellane*, Milano 1880², fig. 234.

Facing page:
Prototype of the chandelier.
Sesto Fiorentino, Museo Richard-Ginori
della Manifattura di Doccia

sisted by the painter Raffaele Faccioli, a young *verista* painter from Bologna, who, almost ten years later, painted the curtain in the Crevalcore theatre. The documents attesting to the formation and development of the "Lodi syle" have gradually been coming to light over the past thirty years: they consist of sketches, drawings, letters, and notes left by Gaetano, kept in public and private collections in Bologna, Crevalcore, and Florence. To these we can add the photographs of the Giza Palace kept in the archives of the University of Milan, and the above mentioned watercolors. Additionally, in the archives of Lodi's heirs, forty-seven letters written by him from Cairo between mid 1872 and the beginning of 1877 – some of them addressed to Luigi Vassalli – have been found, together with a list of the works executed in Egypt.

Like Ambroise Baudry, who had became the architect in chief for the Khedive, Gaetano too worked in various buildings and villas in Egypt, decorating them in his very typical style. In 1873, for example, he lived for a while in the Cairo house of a certain Pietro Cicolani from Livorno, and decorated some of his properties, as revealed in a letter dated January 19 of that year.

From his arrival in Cairo, Lodi worked on the creation of the Khedive table service in Egyptian style. This followed a trend starting in the beginning of the nineteenth century, soon after Bonaparte's expedition to Egypt, for porcelain services made in Sèvres, such as that of the Russian Tsar in 1808, or the one for Josephine finished in 1812, and then offered to the duke of Wellington in 1818. This fashion continued until recent times, for example, note Mattheo Thun's "Nefertiti tea set" or his "Teje and Tuja" flower vases designed for the Memphis Design Group in 1981.

The Khedive Ismail commissioned the famous Italian company Ginori, based in Doccia near Florence, to make the service. In a letter to Vassalli, dated August 7, 1872, Gaetano writes that he is preparing the sketches and watercolors for "saliere, zuppiere, piatti da portata" that were shown to the Khedive for approval before being sent to Italy through the Italian consul Giuseppe De Martino. In these true works of art, Gaetano proves his wide knowledge of ancient Egyptian themes and decorative patterns. Once they arrived in Doccia, the drawings and watercolors were transposed into very similar porcelain forms by Jafet Torelli, chief of sculptors, helped by his assistants Vannini and Cesari. The vividly colored decoration of the forms was executed by Leopoldo Nincheri, Lorenzo Becheroni Junior, and Giuseppe Bendassi. As Luigi Figuier wrote in the second edition of his *Le meraviglie dell'industria. Il vetro e le porcellane* (Milan 1880), the "grandioso servizio da tavola in porcellana fu compiuto nel 1875 con somma soddisfazione di quanti lo videro".

We can now affirm, without doubt, that the design of the porcelain State service of Khedive Ismail is thanks to Gaetano Lodi. The twenty-five watercolors offered for study to the Egyptological Archives of the University of Milan, together with the one kept in the Cooper-Hewitt Museum in New York City, are almost identical to the porcelain objects produced by Ginori, whose prototypes are now kept in the Museo Richard-Ginori della Manifattura di Doccia. The table centerpiece consists of a large shallow bowl resting on blue hippopotami, shown in side and end view in the New York watercolor. It was made in the mid 1870s, and is apparently not present in the Doccia Collection. This centerpiece, as well as many other objects, was actually photographed by the renowned Luigi Montabone before 1877, the year of his death. Montabone was active in Turin, where he worked for the

94

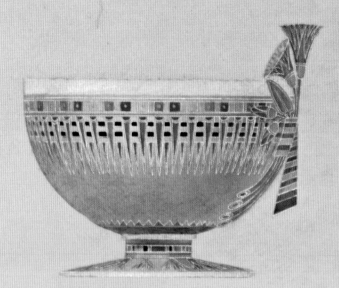

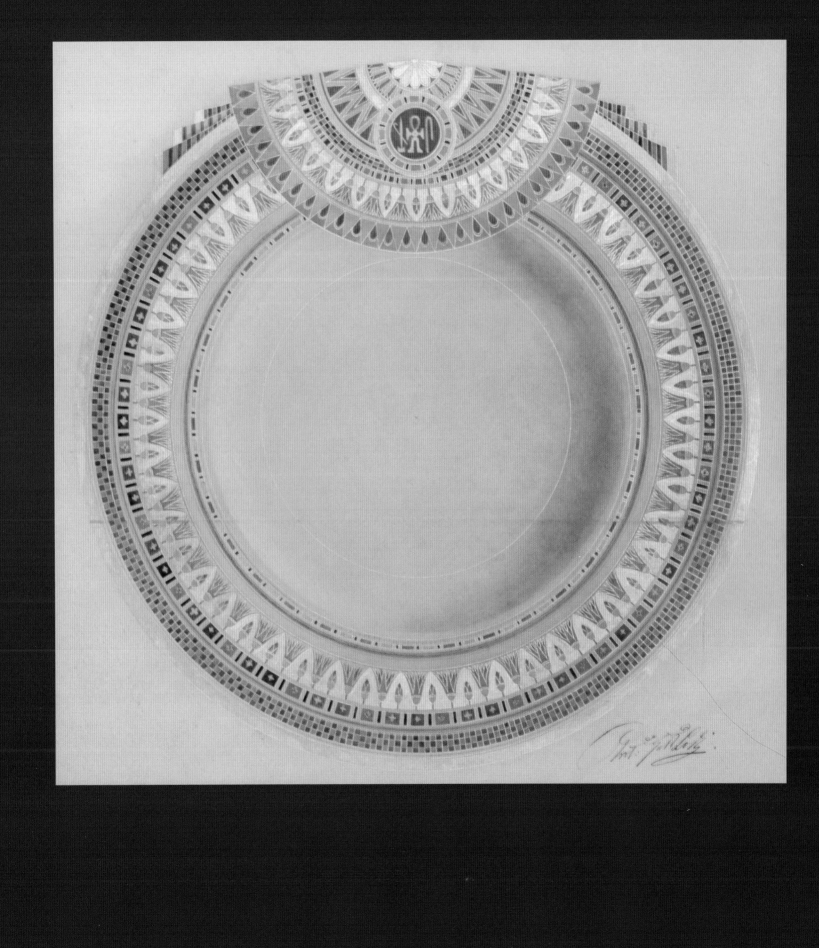

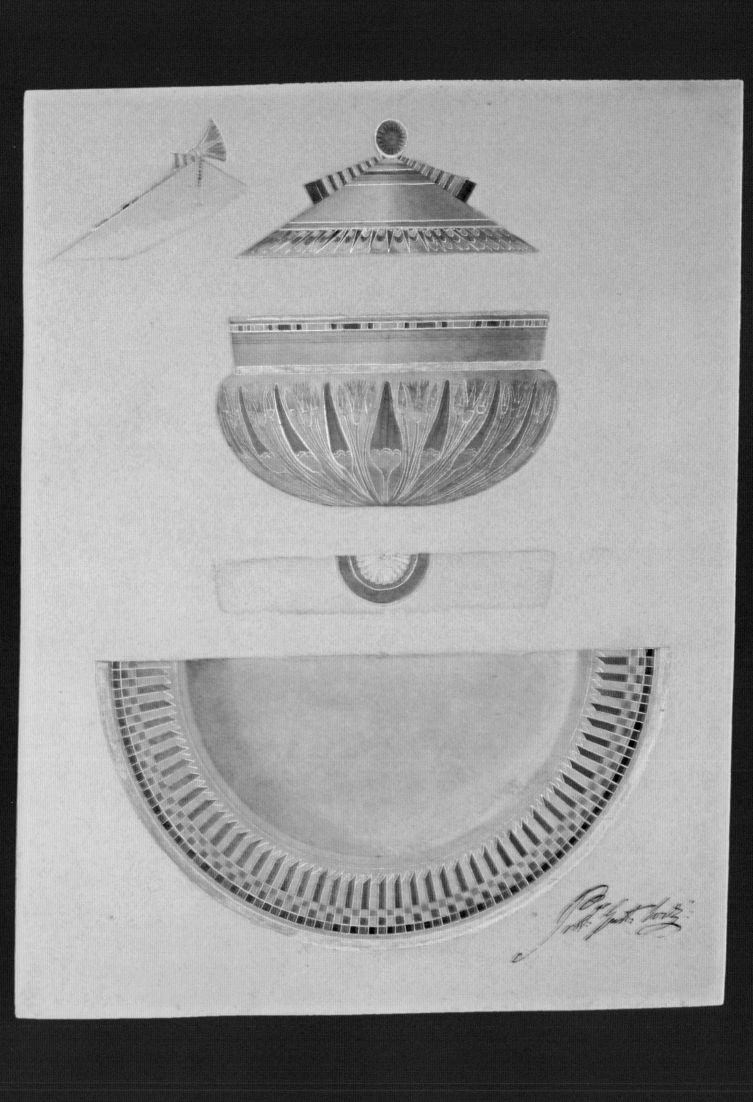

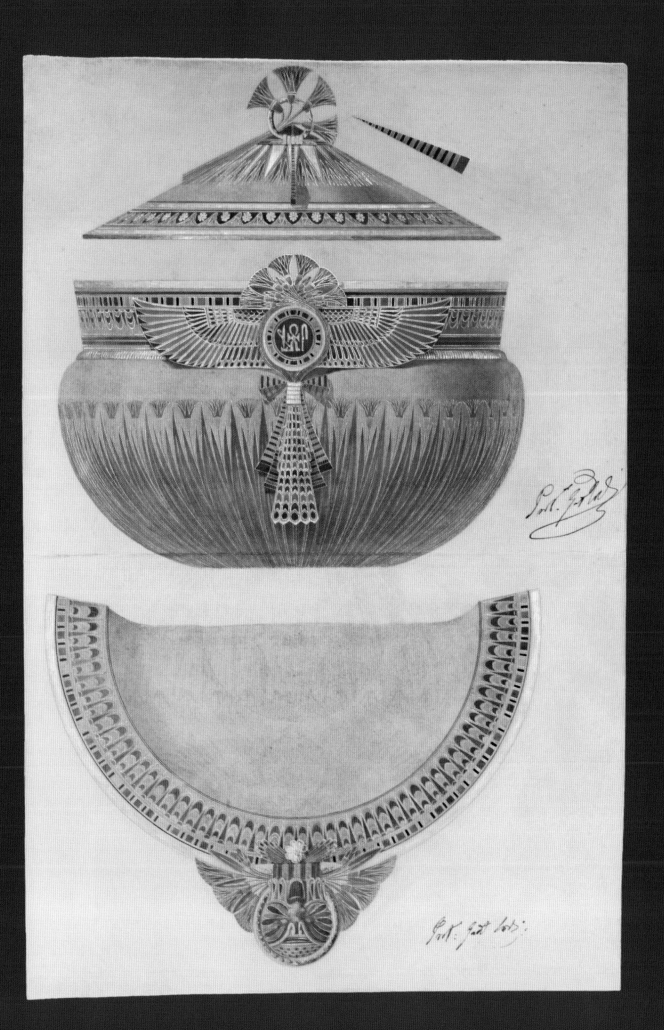

King, but he also worked in Milan, Florence, and even in Cairo. Thus he could have met Lodi on several different occasions, and it's probably not by chance that he was chosen to reproduce the main pieces of Ismail's service designed by Gaetano Lodi. Twenty-eight of Montabone's photographs of the service are now kept in the archives of the Museo Ginori in Doccia. In addition, the drawings of some objects were reproduced in *Le meraviglie dell'industria. Il vetro e le porcellane* by Figuier. For the chandelier, for example, we have now located the original watercolor by Lodi (private collection, temporarily housed in the University of Milan), the real object with some variations from the original design (Museo Ginori), the photograph by Montabone (archives of the Museo Ginori), and a drawing (reproduced in Figuier's book).

On July 9, 1875, the Direttore generale del Ministero dell'Educazione, Giuseppe Fiorelli, sent a letter to Lodi to thank him for having created a series of plaster casts of ancient-Egyptian reliefs and stelae, which were then sent to the Museo Archeologico in Florence. Lodi thus made an important contribution to the diffusion and development of Egyptology in Italy. Other casts of Egyptian monuments had arrived in the Museo Archeologico in Naples in 1874, but we do not know whether Lodi was the author. Some years before, in 1871, Luigi Vassalli had already made casts of monuments kept in the Bulaq Museum, with the help of Michel Ange Floris who executed the work. Cesare Correnti and the Italian government commissioned these reproductions of Egyptian monuments to increase the collection in the Museo Archeologico in Florence. Since Vassalli and Lodi both had close ties from the beginning of the Seventies, it is possible that they worked together on this commission when they were both in Cairo. I am investigating this further.

Between 1874 and 1876, Lodi returned to Italy a few times, where he accepted some minor commissions in Crevalcore and Bologna, and followed the production of Ismail's service in Doccia. In August 1875, during one of his trips, he married Maria Messeri in Florence, and went back to Cairo with her. Here, she gave birth to their first son, Luigi Scipione. Their second son, Cesare Francesco, was born in Bologna, as well as their third baby, Linda Maddalena Maria, who died when she was only twenty-four days old.

In 1876, Gaetano was still living in Cairo, as proved by the certificate issued by the Italian Consulate in Cairo, while his family was already resident in Bologna. This was a year of financial difficulty for Lodi as the government did not pay him for his work, as had also happened to Ambroise Baudry. Gaetano's concerns appear in many of the letters that he wrote to various people, now kept in his family archives. In one of them, sent to a certain Mr Busi, he wrote: "[…] Le commissioni erano però in altri termini, ora tutto è speculazione […] ma in un modo che l'artista vero non può vivere e ti dirò francamente che non veggo l'ora di aver terminato i miei impegni per tornarmene in Italia". In the end, he left the country in January 1877, after he had received numerous offers of work in Italy.

Meanwhile, the Khedive's porcelain service was the subject of a curious story that I am still trying to reconstruct. Ismail Pasha was burdened with debts following the construction of his sumptuous palaces and villas, organizing extraordinary ceremonies to accompany the opening of the Suez Canal in 1869, creating an Opera House in Cairo, commissioning Giuseppe Verdi to compose *Aida*, and so on. In the second half of the Seventies, unable to pay his debts, he was forced to sell the stocks of the Suez Canal, and had to abdicate in 1879. Four years

Large table centerpiece with hippopotami.
Drawing, in L.G. FIGUIER, *Le meraviglie dell'industria. Il vetro e le porcellane*, Milano 1880², fig. 235.

Facing page:
Large table centerpiece with hippopotami.
Watercolor by Gaetano Lodi.
New York City, Cooper-Hewitt Museum

Previous pages:
Gaetano Lodi, selection of preparatory watercolors for the porcelain service of the Khedive Ismail Pasha, 1872-1874.
Private Collection

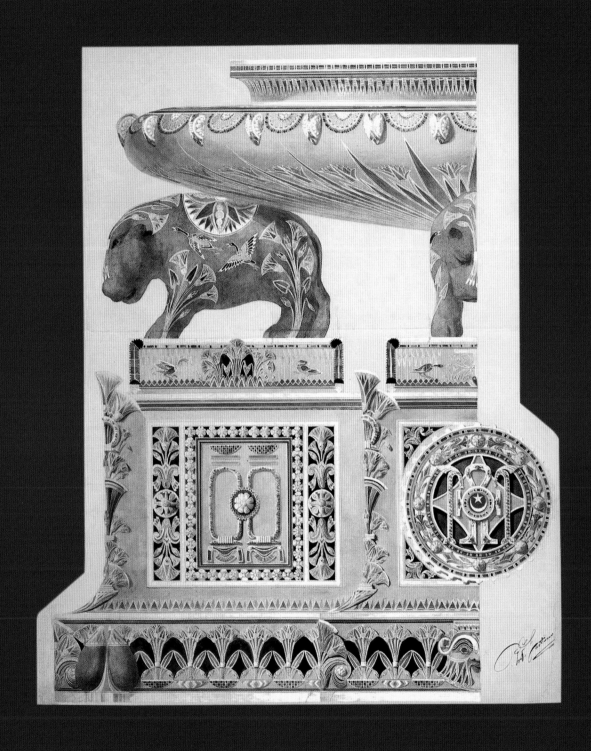

before, from October 20 to 26, 1875, the Prince of Wales, future King Edward VII, stopped in Egypt on his way to India. During the last week of March 1876, Prince Edward stopped again in Egypt, on his return journey to England. During one of these two stays, the Khedive probably offered him the porcelain service designed by Gaetano Lodi, for which he had yet to fully pay Ginori. We gathered this information from two articles, the first published in the *New Zealand Tablet* on February 6, 1880, but dated December 18, 1879: "Ismail Pasha some years ago ordered a magnificent dinner service of porcelain from the firm Ginori of Florence. The price was 100,000 francs, part of which was paid. The dinner service was presented by the Khedive to H.R.H. the Prince of Wales. The Marquis Ginori now sues the ex-Khedive for 76,100 francs, the unpaid balance of his account."

As we have already mentioned, Ismail Pasha abdicated in 1879, and found hospitality in the Borbone's Villa della Favorita in Naples. To receive payment, Ginori took his case to tribunal. The designated law officer, unable to enter the securely locked and protected property, found a very original way of presenting the order to the Khedive. He waited in the street for the Khedive, who came out every day for a tour in his elegant chariot. As soon as the official saw the chariot, he threw the statement of liquidated claim, which landed on Ismail's knees. He could no longer ignore the request, and was obliged to pay. In another article published on the *New Zealand Tablet* on May 21, 1880, we can read: "The Marquis Ginori, proprietor of the Florence Porcelain Works, has gained judgement in the Naples Court against the ex-Khedive for the sum due for dinner service ordered by the latter, and presented by him to the Prince of Wales."

Research undertaken in the Royal Collection in London, and in the Royal Archives in Windsor, has been unfruitful, since no pieces from that porcelain service, nor information on the Khedive's gift to Prince Edward, have been found. But further research will hopefully help us to discover whether the service was really offered to the Prince, as seems to be the case according to the press of the time, and to find out its location.

Another very important work by Lodi in "Egyptianizing" style was discovered in Bologna in 1986, during the renovation of Palazzo Sanguinetti in Strada Maggiore; the palazzo was named after the banker Angelo Sanguinetti from Modena, who bought it in 1870. It consists of the complete decoration of the Saletta Egizia, almost unknown in any literature relating to the painter, and completely ignored in studies on the Egyptian Revival. Sanguinetti commissioned Lodi a few years after he had returned from Egypt, perhaps in 1881 despite the fact that some of Lodi's sketches, dating back to 1879, show a series of Egyptian motifs that are present in the decoration of the Saletta Egizia – two sketches are published in the catalogue of the exhibition devoted to Lodi in Crevalcore in 1987. There is a possibility that the plans were conceived earlier, and only implemented by Gaetano at the beginning of the Eighties. The frescos, completely inspired by ancient-Egyptian themes, show deities, animals and human beings as well as typical Nilotic landscape. The decorations of this building represent one of the most significant examples of the eclectic art of the nineteenth century in Bologna, in which neoclassical themes are mixed with Egyptian ones. Since the first half of the century, the palace was decorated in different revival styles, from neoclassical to neo-Etruscan and neo-Pompeian. One of its first decorators was Pelagio Palagi, the renowned Bolognese

Fig. 257. Ampolliera pel Kedivé (fabbrica Ginori).

Fig. 256. Coppa per frutta (fabbrica Ginori).

Oil and vinegar cruet. Drawing, in L.G. FIGUIER, *Le meraviglie dell'industria. Il vetro e le porcellane*, Milano 1880², fig. 237.

Fruit dish. Drawing, in L.G. FIGUIER, *Le meraviglie ...* cit. Milano 1880², fig. 236.

Facing page and following pages:
Gaetano Lodi, selection of preparatory watercolors for the porcelain service of the Khedive Ismail Pasha, 1872-1874.
Private Collection

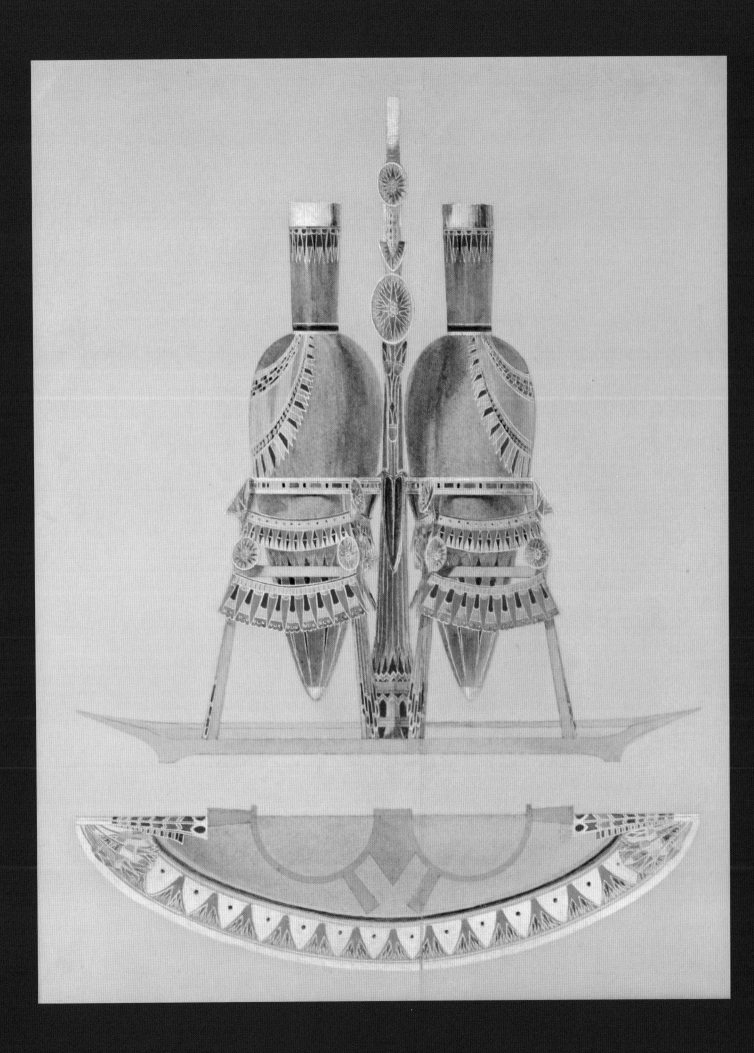

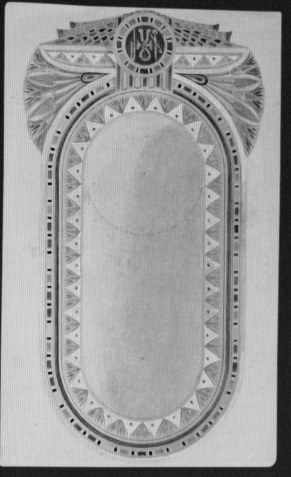

Modello n° 2

Prof. Gaetano Lodi

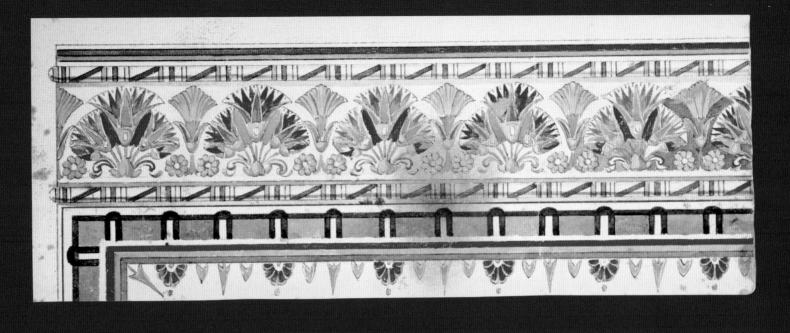

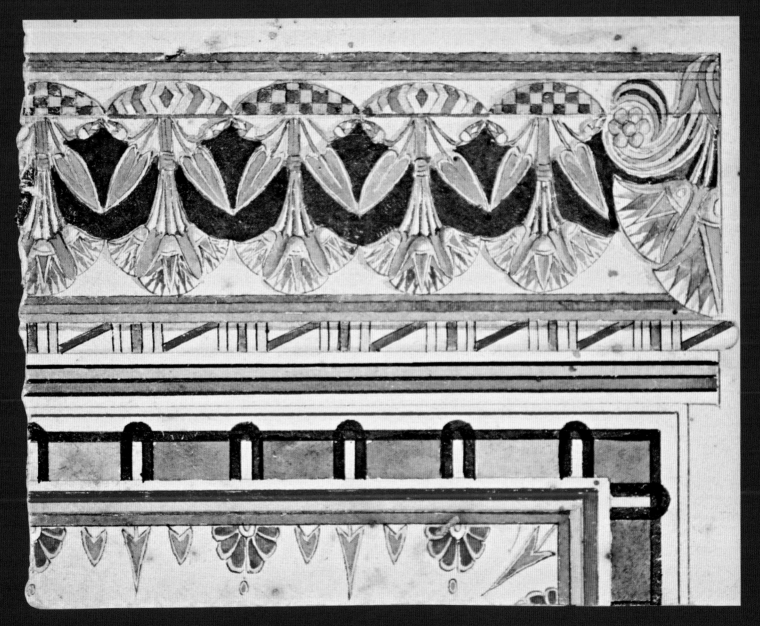

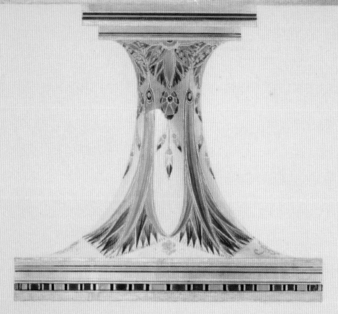

artist and collector who had a taste for classical and Egyptian art.

During the same years 1878-81, Gaetano Lodi worked in Creval-core again, this time on the new design of the local theatre. An oriental-style flamered floral composition covers the interior, achieving its greatest effect on the ceiling.

Lodi eventually became Professore di Ornato at the Accademia di Belle Arti, as mentioned above, and from 1882 taught the theory and practice of decoration to young painters and craftsmen in the Cooperativa Ceramica d'Imola. This is supported by a series of very interesting notes recently discovered in the archives in Crevalcore. From July 1883 until his death, in 1886, Gaetano was the Direttore artistico of the Cooperativa. Some dishes in "Egyptianizing" style date back to these years and are very similar to those made ten years earlier for the Khedive's service, but with which they should not be confused. The series produced in Imola bears the name of the town, or the symbol of the Cooperativa, or the arms of Crevalcore, as well as the date on the back, while Lodi's signature can be on the front or on the back.

Another "Egyptianizing" series was produced in Doccia after 1907, in the factory then called Richard-Ginori, after the fusion with Giulio Richard's Milanese factory in 1896. Its design, inspired by Lodi, was made by Sem Bini in December 1907 and called "Servito Ricordi Faraone". A large round plate, not yet painted but moulded with three lotus flowers, a winged sun, and a knot in relief on the top edge, appeared on the antiquities market in May 2010. In the auction catalogue, it was described as a possible prototype for the Khedive's service. However, it has to be attributed to the later "Servito Ricordi Faraone", in which we can actually see the same motifs in relief. In addition, an identical large round plate, with identical motifs but with a painted edge, is kept in the collection of the Museo Richard-Ginori della Manifattura di Doccia, where it has been attributed to the Sem Bini's series as well.

Portrait of Gaetano Lodi. Photograph.
Private Collection

Facing page:
Gaetano Lodi, preparatory watercolor
for the porcelain service of the Khedive Ismail Pasha,
1872-1874.
Private Collection

Following pages:
Palazzo Sanguinetti.
Palazzo già Riario Sforza ora Donzelli in Bologna,
V. Vegetti dis., L. Paradisi inc., in "Almanacco statistico bolognese", 1835, p. 133.
Bologna, Biblioteca dell'Archiginnasio

Saletta Egizia decorated by Gaetano Lodi,
Palazzo Sanguinetti, Bologna.
Bologna, Museo Internazionale e Biblioteca della Musica

Detail of the Saletta Egizia decorated by Gaetano Lodi,
Palazzo Sanguinetti, Bologna.
Bologna, Museo Internazionale e Biblioteca della Musica

V. Vegetti dis.   L. Paradisi in.

PALAZZO GIA RIARIO SFORZA ORA DONZELLI IN BOLOGNA

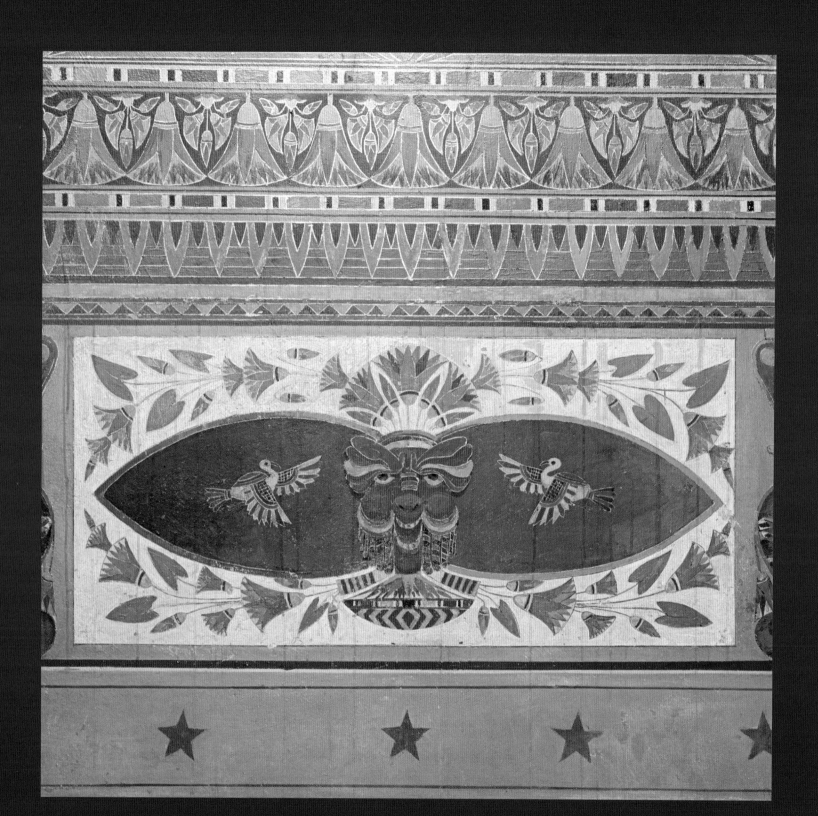

Egypt as an Allegory of the Modern Age

Political Satire, Illustration and Imagérie populaire

Antonello Negri, Marta Sironi

V. *Egypt as an Allegory of the Modern Age*

Political Satire, Illustration and Imagérie populaire

Antonello Negri, Marta Sironi

When publishing and illustration were becoming increasingly industrialized from the 1830s onward – combined with the growing fashion for popular or political cartoons and illustrations for children – ancient Egypt and its civilization were reinvented, or rather synthesized, through recurrent icons linked to Egypt's monuments (pyramids, sphinxes, and temples), its flora and fauna (palms, papyrus, crocodiles, and camels), the postures of men and women in the prevalent iconography, and the apparently mysterious hieroglyphic inscriptions. All of these elements were ideal for contributing, through cleverly contrived visual reconstructions, to the success of an adventure literature in search of amazing, strange, and frightening tales.

The trend is exemplified in the drawings of the French artist Grandville. They show how a fashion dating back several decades was, in the new bourgeois society, just one among many possible stylistic choices. In *Un autre monde* (Paris 1844), written and illustrated by Grandville himself, the artist makes fun of this interchangeability of styles, and compares it to that of exchanging goods in the new global market. One example is an illustration in which a typical, humanized Egyptian divinity – a human figure with the head of a bird – is placed in a modern urban context. On its head it balances a metal receptacle, a sort of cross between a canopic jar and a milk churn, in its hand it carries an oil lamp, and it wears a pair of Dutch-style clogs on its feet, evoking an antelucan service in a still sleeping city. All around are typical urban furnishings: a beautiful Baroque-like fountain, a cast iron lamp stand, and an obelisk. The idea is still that of modernity as a place of systematic contamination of the past in all its forms and manifestations – stretching back from the Baroque period to the Egyptian civilization – and of the present. Grandville returns to the obelisk theme in a drawing that illustrates – in a suitably enigmatic way – the presumed mystery of hieroglyphic writing, a cliché for enigma. The drawing shows a man – an *imbécile* in the text – striking his head against an obelisk covered in inscriptions and figures, because he is unable to understand them – but at the end of the book Grandville gives the solution to the puzzle, because it is a puzzle itself that is engraved on the obelisk in the form of obscure hieroglyphs.

Next to the obelisk with its hieroglyphs stands another commonplace of Egyptian civilization: the pyramid. It is featured in an illustration suggesting unexpected combinations between the wonders of the mineral world and forms apparently invented only by man, yet themselves actually inspired by that very world. Thus, alongside forests of obelisks and pyramids, we find the pointed arches and spires of the Gothic cathedrals, dice, halberds, and sugar loaves, in a surreal interplay of mirrors in which nature and artifice are reflected.

Facing page:
GRANDVILLE, "… cette petite latière de Memphis, gracieuse comme un ibis, légère comme une gazelle", in *Un autre monde*, Paris 1844, p. 205.

GRANDVILLE, "… il faudrait placer en tête d'Un Autre Monde le rébus suivant", in *Un autre monde*, Paris 1844, p. 290.

GRANDVILLE, "Plantes marines, coquillages, madrépores", in *Un autre monde*, Paris 1844, p. 119.

The story illustrated by Grandville may seem banal but actually it is sharp and revealing, which is why the French poet Charles Baudelaire, and later the Surrealists, loved it. It was also one of the starting points for a minor trend in graphic design which went through a number of divergences and variants of Egyptomania during the second half of the nineteenth century, eventually finding its way into the more trivial forms of iconography of the twentieth century, a century characterized by the diffusion of all kinds of ideas and images at every level.

In the satirical graphics of the nineteenth century, in particular in Italy, Egyptian *imagérie* corresponds to the idea of something ancient, unchanging, and it is a metaphor that fits well with the stagnation of certain politics of the time. Egyptian vignettes started to appear sporadically in 1848, but it was the Italian artist Casimiro Teja who first produced a coherent and extended series of drawings, motivated primarily by the climate generated when the isthmus of Suez was at the center of international controversy. Stylistically, Teja was influenced by graphic models from beyond the Alps, notably those published in London's *Punch* magazine, where the most important illustrators liked to vary their usual style by imitating "primitive" art. The most famous examples are the Japanese style of Harry Furniss (under the pseudonym Laka Joko) and the Babylonian style of Edward Tennyson Reed. The same device was cleverly employed by Teja, who, in the 1870s, was still practically the only illustrator for *Pasquino*. The Egyptian style was not only a visually effective way of commenting on contemporary political events, but it also allowed Teja to introduce a graphic variation into the pages of the satirical weekly, making it more interesting for readers. The Egyptian take on current affairs was particularly appreciated by readers in Turin, thanks to the presence of the Egyptian Museum, founded in 1824. However, the main incentive for such a large Egyptian series came from the artist's participation in the international delegation of journalists invited to the sumptuous festivities for the inauguration of the Suez Canal in November and December 1869.

The first article in *Pasquino*, "L'istmo di Suez", was published in 1869. It is almost a live account, followed immediately by an album intended as a New Year's gift for subscribers:

Il viaggio in Oriente ha ispirato all'artista le pagine di questo *Album* nel quale usi, costumi, personaggi importanti, monumenti, paesi, tutto insomma è rappresentato umoristicamente; sarà l'unica pubblicazione fatta in Europa su questo tema ed in questo genere. Il pubblico vedrà in tavole artistiche ed eleganti il paragone tra la civiltà degli antichi e quella dei moderni, tra la civiltà dei beduini e quella degli europei.

In these elegant illustrations readers will be able to observe the differences between the ancient civilization and the modern one, between the civilization of the Bedouins and that of the Europeans.

The episodes illustrated in both cases are the same ones described by Teja's colleague, the journalist Giuseppe Augusto Cesana in his volume of memoirs of the same trip, entitled *Da Firenze a Suez e viceversa* (Florence 1870), where details of contemporary political issues are merged with the events of everyday life, and where the journalist – like Teja in *Pasquino* – portrays himself and his traveling companions, all well-known to the readers, whose adventures give the story a more direct, almost familial appeal. The *Album*'s cover immediately summarizes the main features of the series: on one side we can see ancient Egypt (through the architectural detail of an ancient temple), on

Facing page:
C. Teja, *Pasquino | all'Istmo di Suez | Album,* Torino 1870.

C. Teja, "Nella terra dei Faraoni", in *Pasquino* (2/3/1879). Centro Apice, Marengo Collection

C. Teja, "L'Italia in Egitto e viceversa", in *Pasquino* (13/4/1879). Centro Apice, Marengo Collection

120

Nella terra dei Faraoni

I rappresentanti di JOHN BULL e di JEAN BONHOMME incaricati di studiare l'amministrazione egiziana vi trovano qualche difficoltà essendo espressa in troppi geroglifici.

L'ITALIA IN EGITTO E VICEVERSA

the other the modern political question (a view of the Canal works). Teja himself is a key figure in the adventure, pictured as he embarks on the ship *Italia* on the first page of *Pasquino* or in Arab dress as he puts the finishing touches to his work, signing the cover of the *Album*. In order to vary the narrative and make it easier to read, Teja breaks the rhythm of the illustrations by using an "archaeological" style in the central strip, inspired by the bas-reliefs of Saqqara. It is actually a fairly obvious reference to Italian politics, where the "Menabrea-Digny couple" represent the brief tenure of the Menabrea government (October 27, 1867-January 5, 1868), in which the Minister of Finance was in fact Guglielmo Cambray Digny.

After this first series of drawings in 1869, completed when the memory of the trip was still fresh, Egyptian cartoons continued to appear, especially with reference to the political question. The protagonist was Ismail Pasha, Khedive of Egypt. Teja constructed a real cartoon character around this key figure in Egyptian politics of the time: a portly pharaoh who loves the splendors of the ancient civilization, always caught thumbing his nose at the European powers – France and England in particular – which laid down the law like a latter-day Moses. In 1879 the Egyptian economic crisis worsened, and French and English politicians and administrators were called in to act as bankruptcy receivers. One of Teja's caricatures shows them trying to decipher the hieroglyphs of the administration. This was the moment for the second Egyptian series, which transformed the international question into street entertainment. In *Al Gran Teatro Egitto*, the Khedive plays a big drum, calling upon the European creditors to watch the show. At his side, as if in a stage backdrop, England and France are outlined against the figures carved on the monuments of ancient Egypt. The caption announces an interesting show with an uncertain outcome: will Egypt drown in a sea of debt or will it be the European creditors that drown?

As the Egyptian situation deteriorated, the idea of an Italian intervention began to take shape. Teja's response was one of his most successful plates: how can Italy, which is full of political mummies, intervene? With a caption that recalls Cesana's title – *Dall'Italia all'Egitto e viceversa* – the leader of the Left, Depretis, then in power, is depicted full page as an Egyptian colossus, with the fiascos of his policies – the Stradella program and the defeat of Lissa – clearly visible among the hieroglyphs on the wall behind him.

Without wishing to undermine their achievements, it is undeniable that the above artists were involved in a rather light-hearted sphere of production. It should not be forgotten that during the same period, works of a higher cultural quality were being produced by two schools of graphic art in France and Germany, not as important as the *Belle Époque* but nevertheless significant. In the magazine *Jugend*, published in Munich, Julius Diez uses Egypt as a starting point in his article on the history of cycling through the ages, inventing witty parallels between customs, behaviour, and language. In France, meanwhile, inventive artists like Charles Léandre, Lucien Métivet, and Albert Robida – who in his Parisian *Arabian Nights* unfolds a whole repertoire of images, figures, and situations worthy of a Hollywood blockbuster – provided another splendid magazine, *Le Rire*, with color plates humorously interpreting Egypt, its personalities, stories, and forms, in the new *Art Nouveau* style then very much in vogue.

At the root of the iconography that reinvents ancient Egypt in satirical graphic art and illustration for adults and children is the Ori-

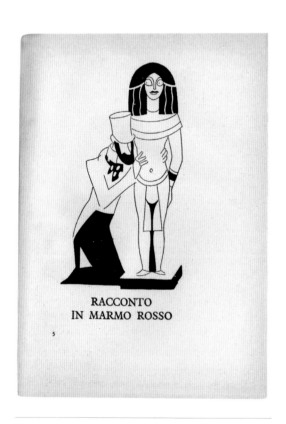

RACCONTO
IN MARMO ROSSO

M. Pompei, "Racconto in Marmo rosso",
in E. Giovannetti, *Sirene in vacanza*, Roma 1927.
Centro Apice, Sergio Reggi '900 Collection

Facing page:
J. Diez, "Entwickelung des Radfahrsports durch
die Jahrhunderte", in *Jugend* (4/9/1897), pp. 602-603.
Centro Apice, Marengo Collection

L. Métivet, "Les belles dames. Madame Putiphar",
in *Le Rire* (14/3/1896), p. 12.
Centro Apice, Marengo Collection

G. Staal, "Isis et Osiris, Les femmes mythologiques",
in J. Méry et le c.te Foelix, *Muses et fées, histoire
des femmes mythologiques*, Paris [1851].
Centro Apice, Alfieri Collection

Aus dem culturgeschichtlichen Bilderbuch der „Jugend":

LES BELLES DAMES
III. — MADAME PUTIPHAR

MADAME PUTIPHAR. — Quelle veste! C'est pas même un demi-vierge!
JOSEPH (hurlant). — Maman! maman! la dame m'a chipé mon smoking!

Dessin de L. Mocmet.

MUSES ET FÉES.

IRIS ET OSIRIS.

entalist pictorial tradition, which turned its attention to Egypt throughout the nineteenth century, starting from the rediscovery of the country linked to the Napoleonic campaign and their aftermath.

In earlier painting, Egyptian themes featured in works with biblical scenes. For example, in the seventeenth-century version of *Moïse sauvé des eaux* by Nicolas Poussin, the painter uses the image of the pyramid to locate the viewers immediately, conforming to a common practise whereby the iconographic attribute allows instant recognition of the context: pyramids and sphinxes, crocodiles and camels, between *High and Low*, to quote the title of a famous New York exhibition on the typical contradiction of modern art. Starting with Poussin, it is possible to see how the Camel cigarette pack came about by means of a concatenation of trivializations, reflections, and migrations of images and forms, influenced significantly by avant-garde Dadaism – best represented in painting by the German Otto Dix – which itself stems partly from popular graphics and illustration.

Returning to the tradition of nineteenth-century illustration, the visual extremes of large-scale pictorial communication using Egypt as a metaphor can also be identified in the definition of precise iconographic standards. The typical image of Isis and Osiris, for example, which was initially represented with obvious reference to operatic stage sets – such as Staal's illustration for *Muses et fées: histoire des femmes mythologiques* – led gradually to more natural versions. A notable example, for its graphic quality, is the illustration "Marmo rosso" by Mario Pompei.

This tradition spread dramatically with the mass publishing of illustrated material. A typical case – studied by Paola Pallottino – is that of Alberto Della Valle's drawings for Emilio Salgari's novel *Le figlie dei Faraoni* (1906). The end result, an illustrated plate to accompany the text, is a highly effective combination of well-established Orientalist excesses – landscape backgrounds with the usual pyramids and sphinxes, palms and crocodiles, interiors with architectural reconstructions based on the by then well-known graphic reproductions of Egyptian antiquities – also using *tableau vivant* studio reconstructions, which to us may appear grotesque but were extremely useful when, frozen by the camera, they became fundamental structural components of the artist's design. In the Italian context, Della Valle is a typical example of an illustrator who used a naturalistic style. A few decades later, abstraction and the conceptual nature of Egyptian visual culture as perceived by western culture at the time, fitted in well with the thinking of artist-illustrators who were attentive to avant-garde artistic experimentation as well as sensitive to radical simplifications, which communicated particularly effectively. This can be seen in Toddi's illustrations for "I capricci della principessa Marabù", and in Angoletta's cover for *Giro giro tondo*, where the figures and style have an Egyptian imprint.

In conclusion, let us remember the delightful story, "La piramide di re Piramidone", by Sergio Tofano, the famous Sto of *Signor Bonaventura*, who uses verse and illustration to tell the tale of an amazing adventure set in ancient Egypt. The story unfolds as a series of scenes as in avant-garde Dada-Surrealist contemporary cinema. It is in line with the early attempts by Disney and others to produce animated cartoons with a spectacular *finale*. Obviously there is a happy ending, after a somewhat bittersweet beginning, playing on the idea of the least cheerful aspect of the pyramid. The Egypt imagined by Blechman, the American inventor of illustrated stories, is very different. He deals with the biblical theme of the flight into Egypt in a comic and ironic way.

Alberto Della Valle's studio. Photograph, in P. Pallottino (ed.), *L'occhio della tigre. Alberto Della Valle fotografo e illustratore salgariano*, Palermo 1994.

Facing page:
A. Della Valle, "... era sorta improvvisamente una giovane donna, di bellezza meravigliosa", in E. SALGARI, *Le figlie dei Faraoni*, Genova 1906. Centro Apice, Sergio Reggi '900 Collection

Following pages:
B. Angoletta, *Giro giro tondo* (1/5/1923). Cover. Centro Apice, Sergio Reggi '900 Collection

E. Toddi, "I capricci della principessa Marabù", in C. PIMPA LEO, *I fiori nel pozzo*, Bologna 1921. Centro Apice, Sergio Reggi '900 Collection

STO, "La piramide di re Piramidone", in ID., *Storie di cantastorie*, Firenze [1923]. Centro Apice, Sergio Reggi '900 Collection

R.O. Blechman, *Tutto esaurito*, [Milano] 1971. Centro Apice, Grandini Collection

..... era sorta improvvisamente una giovane donna, di bellezza
meravigliosa. *(Cap. IX.)*.

(I capricci della principessa Marabù)

.... chiamò i suoi schiavetti, fece aprire il cofano e trarre fuori lo specchio.

"Quando il re Piramidone
che l'Egitto governava
di sposare ebbe intenzione
una moglie onesta e brava,
impalmò Melchisedecca
principessa della Mecca,
donna ricca di virtù,
bella e ricca per di più
[...]
Possedea Piramidone
la piramide più bella
per ricchezza
e dimensione dell'Egitto:
ed era quella un sol blocco
di granito
di topazî rivestito;
dentro tutto un luccicor
di fantastici tesor.
Ma la sposa
in quella casa …
niente casa e tutto tetto,
da tristezza grande è invasa
che la fa languire in letto.
La piramide gigante
sul suo cuor
com'è pesante!
Un palazzo non le par
ma una tomba d'abitar."

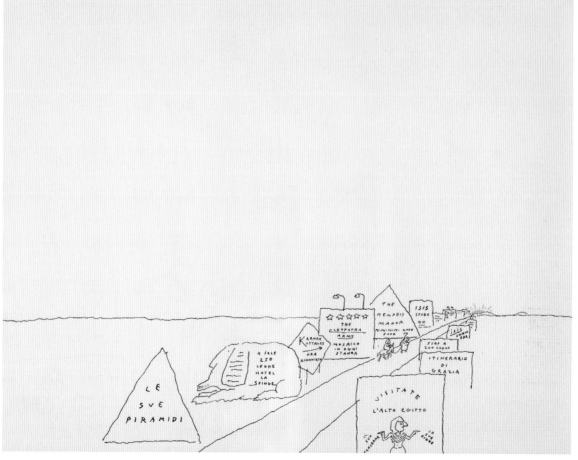

Egypt in the Box
Pharaonic Inspiration in Everyday Life

Patrizia Piacentini

VI. *Egypt in the Box*

Pharaonic Inspiration in Everyday Life

Patrizia Piacentini

The Milanese Association *Per-megiat onlus per la tutela e la valorizzazione delle biblioteche sull'antico Egitto* deposited a very special collection in the Egyptological Archives of the University of Milan for study purposes. It consists of a group of more than eight hundred items inspired by ancient Egypt, most of which are cigarette boxes decorated with "Egyptianizing" images: pyramids and temples, sphinxes and exotic animals, pharaohs, and sexy queens. Some of these boxes were shown for the first time at the exhibition *Il Tesoro della Statale. Collezioni e identità di un grande Ateneo*, organized by the University of Milan, and held there from November 2004 to February 2005.

These objects are among the most recent expressions of a fashion trend that has its roots in imperial Rome, and flourished in the Renaissance up until today. Waves of Egyptomania are known in the relatively recent history of taste, which coincide with exceptional events relating to Egypt. The first one was the Napoleonic expedition in 1798-99, followed by the opening of the Suez Canal in 1869, the movement of obelisks from Egypt to Paris, London, and New York between 1836 and 1881, and the discovery of the tomb of Tutankhamun in 1922.

The Egyptian style slowly permeated all the forms of architecture and art, satirical journals (see Chapter V), publishing and advertising, theater, music, movies, and all kinds of entertainment, as well as decorative arts. A generally stereotyped image of Egypt spread from high art and culture to the popular level, as expressed in objects used in daily life: containers for talcum powder, cosmetics, and perfumes, tin boxes for cigarettes, chocolate or biscuits, as well as jewellery and women's handbags and clothing, ceramic services from dishes to tea-pots, lamps and decorative objects, door knockers, sewing machines, furniture and pianos, and even trains. For example, the Baldwin locomotives of the early 1870s were decorated with classically inspired linework on the tender sides, arabesques on the dome sides, and Egyptian-inspired motifs on the dome tops, in a kind of Neo-Baroque style in which Gaetano Lodi was a master (see Chapter IV).

The lure of exotic travel in the first decades of the nineteenth century and an ever-widening international base of clients pushed many famous jewelers to produce objects inspired from all parts of the globe. The Egyptomania of the 1920s was put to use immediately at Van Cleef & Arpels, and again in the 1970s when the traveling King Tutankhamun exhibition arrived at the Metropolitan Museum of Art in New York. Among the jewellery of pharaonic inspiration, the 1924 "Egyptian bracelet" by Van Cleef & Arpels, with a soaring bird rendered in emeralds, sapphires, and rubies, is particularly noteworthy. But Egypt was often present in mass-produced series and cheaper jewellery too.

Egypt was, and still is largely used in advertising to give the idea of beauty, duration, and strength, or just to suggest an amusing, light-hearted image. Sometimes an Egyptian theme has been used

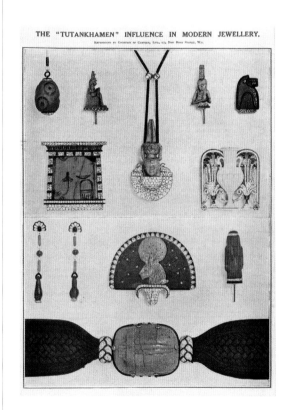

THE "TUTANKHAMEN" INFLUENCE IN MODERN JEWELLERY.

Advertisement from the *Illustrated London News*, 1924, for Cartier Egyptian-style jewellery, captioned "Egyptian trinkets from 1500-3000 years old adapted as modern jewellery: brooches, pendants, earrings and hat-pins set with real antiques."
Eg. Arch. & Lib., Private Collection

Facing page:
Cigars box used by V. Loret to contain lexicographical cards.
Eg. Arch. & Lib., Loret Collection

merely as an eye-catching, easily recognizable icon. A product long connected with the pharaohs' country is Palmolive soap. Made from palm and olive oil, it has been advertized using Egyptian motifs since 1910, a few years after the foundation of the company. Housewives were identified with modern Cleopatras, who could obtain what was "Once a Queen's secret," achieving the "Re-incarnation of Beauty." Today, one can still purchase Palmolive soap in France or in eastern Mediterranean countries under the name of *Cleopatra soap*. Egypt frequently featured on the sets of collectible trade cards offered with Liebig's meat extract from 1867; they were often designed by a famous artist and were first produced using lithography, then chromolithography.

The same methods were used to produce fancy cigarette box labels in Egyptian style. This became prominent with the establishment of tobacco production or marketing in Egypt. When Mohamed Aly, who had been a tobacco trader in Kavalla, assumed power in Egypt in 1805, he aspired to modernize the state in every way. The cultivation of tobacco was among the innovations that he introduced. The first plantations yielded excellent quantitative results, but a product of very low quality. Various attempts to obtain a better and more lucrative product continued under the Khedive Ismail Pasha; however, tobacco cultivation was banned by law in 1883 in favor of trade. The Egyptian government imposed custom duties on imported tobacco and established large warehouses in Alexandria and Cairo, subletting them to manufacturers and traders. Most of them were Greeks, who had left Turkey for Egypt in the second half of the 1870s. In 1884, a commercial trade agreement was signed between Greece and Egypt, which gave Greek tobacco import priority. The Greek factories in Egypt multiplied and improved production and packaging, while their luxurious and expensive cigarettes became one of the most refined products of the time. This impressive success continued until 1913, after which the small tobacco manufactures fell into decline. Later large, modern factories for the production of Egyptian-style cigarettes were established in Germany, England, America, India, and South Africa. Finally, between the World Wars, the Graeco-Egyptian brands disappeared from the marketplace, one after the other, and most cigarette factories closed.

Many elegant and attractive cigarette and cigar boxes were produced in Egypt during the last twenty years of the nineteenth century and the first decades of the twentieth. The boxes were made in cardboard until around 1880, and then in metal with chromolithographed paper labels. From the 1890s, the decoration of the tin boxes was printed directly onto the metal. The production and popularity of this packaging grew after the greatest discoveries were made in the Valley of the Nile, from those of Auguste Mariette at Saqqara in the second half of the nineteenth century to that of the tomb of Tutankhamun in 1922.

The design of some of the labels is directly inspired by famous paintings, photographs, book plates, and archaeological items. On a box of *Ambar Cigarettes*, by Philip E. Mitry, the Giza sphinx and the pyramids seem to be taken from a photograph of the time, probably the same as one of the images sold at the Anglo-American Bookshop located opposite Shepheard's Hotel in Cairo. Both the bookshop and the cigarette brand were owned by the famous dealer and collector of Egyptian antiquities Philip E. Mitry. In the early 1950s, he sold his store and moved to the United States, where his 1100-piece collection was sold in 1996.

The decoration of the cigarette box produced by *Fioravanti*, a

132

company active in Port Said between 1875 and 1935, also seems to come from a photograph.

The decoration of the *Prince of Egypt* cigarette box is directly inspired by the scene of the Asiatics bringing tributes to the pharaoh in the New Kingdom tomb of Amenhotep Huy at Qurnet Murai (TT 40). The *Brera Crüwell-Tabak* tin-box seems to be an animated version of the scene of the pharaoh leaving a temple in his chariot, followed by his attendants. But the pharaoh is substituted on the box by a queen looking like Nefertiti. On the German *Halpaus Aclesto* cigarette box, a coloured façade of the temple of Esna is reproduced with a bit of poetic licence.

The symbol of the *Melachrino* brand – owned by the rich business man Miltiades Melachrino – consists of the three famous statues found by Mariette in the tomb of Psamtek in Saqqara in 1863, representing Isis, Osiris, and Hathor in form of a cow protecting the owner of the tomb. Melachrino had probably seen this amazing group of statues in the Bulaq Museum, and decided to use them as his "intellectual" copyright logo.

Hermes Mixed Egyptian Cigarettes – owned by Chapchal Frères manufacturers in Cairo – have a quasi-real Akhenaton-head represented on the boxes, while one of the ram-headed sphinxes from the Great Temple of Karnak is drawn on the *Freyha Cigarette* box.

The *O'San* cigar box has a beautiful label that combines a great number of ancient and modern Egyptian motifs. The Turkish crescent is the central image but in the background pyramids, camels, and palms are depicted. The foreground design is in an ancient-Egyptian style, with the winged-scarab in the centre and a half-naked Egyptian musician on the left, playing the harp for the queen reclining on the right. Her image is inspired by Cabanel's painting *Cléopatre essayant des poisons sur des condamnés à mort*, 1887 (see Chapter III).

Another amazing tin box is the one produced for the *Record Papier Pour Cigarettes*. This is an excellent example of a large lithographed counter display tin. The top, which shows Cleopatra on her barge on the Nile opposite the pyramids at Giza, as well as all four sides of the box are decorated. The queen's two servants are shown rolling cigarettes and offering them to her. This scene comes directly from Sir Lawrence Alma-Tadema's famous painting *The meeting of Anthony and Cleopatra*, 1883. The boatmen on the left have been replaced with a more iconic view of the pyramids of Giza on the opposite shore, and the two servants duties have shifted from playing music to providing cigarettes.

Facing page, top to bottom, left to right:
Finest handmade | Ambar Cigarettes | Philip E. Mitry | Perfume Dept. | at the Anglo-American Bookshop | Opposite Shepheard's Hotel | Cairo Egypt | Specially Manufactured | in | Cairo Egypt.
Paper lithograph on tin, 15.2 x 7.5 x 2.3 cm.
Per-megiat (Rus E. Gant) Collection

Kais. Kön. Tabak Regie|Egyptische Cigaretten | Dames Dames | Preis per 100 St.
Paper lithograph on tin, 12.5 x 9 x 3 cm.
Per-megiat (Rus E. Gant) Collection

Egyptian Cigarettes | Mignon | No. 1 | Poulides Bros. | Factory and Depot | New York.
Paper lithograph on tin, 13.8 x 7.2 x 3.3 cm.
Per-megiat (Rus E. Gant) Collection

Divina | Säuberli's Cigarettes.
Gebr. Säuberli Cigarettenfabrik Teufenthal Sweiz.
Lithograph on tin, 9 x 7.3 x 1.7 cm.
Per-megiat (Rus E. Gant) Collection

Fioravanti Cigarette Cʸ | Best Egyptian | Cigarettes Manufactory | Port-Said | Egypt.
100 Cigarettes Purveyor to various European royalty and to the Imperial Japanese Government etc., established A.D. 1875.
Lithograph on tin, 14.2 x 9.8 x 3.4 cm.
Per-megiat (Rus E. Gant) Collection

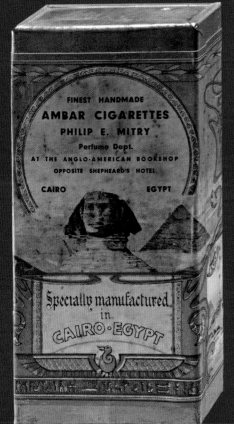

FINEST HANDMADE
AMBAR CIGARETTES
PHILIP E. MITRY
Perfume Dept.
AT THE ANGLO-AMERICAN BOOKSHOP
OPPOSITE SHEPHEARD'S HOTEL
CAIRO   EGYPT

Specially manufactured
in
CAIRO · EGYPT

KAIS. KÖN. TABAK
EGYPTISCHE CIGAR
DAME

DAME
Preis per 100 St.

EGYPTIAN
CIGARETTES
MIGNON

No. I.

POULIDES BROS.

FACTORY AND DEPOT
NewYork

"DIVINA"

SÄUBERLI'S   CIGARETTES

FIORAVANTI CIGARETTE Cy
BEST EGYPTIAN
CIGARETTES MANUFACTORY
PORT-SAID
EGYPT

شركة بخاين فيوراڤانتي
بور سعيد

Facing page, top to bottom:
Extra Fine | Prince of Egypt | Egyptian Cigarettes.
The best Egyptian Cigarettes sold by Smoking Specialty Stores.
Paper lithograph on tin, 14.5 x 7.5 x 2.6 cm.
Per-megiat (Rus E. Gant) Collection

Egyptian Cigarette Company |G.M.B.H. | Berlin-Cairo-Brussels | Egypt.
Paper lithograph on cardboard, 14 x 8 x 3.5 cm.
Per-megiat (Rus E. Gant) Collection

Halpaus | Aclesto.
Cigaretten Fabrik Breslau und Koln, 25 Aclesto Gold Egyptian Cigarettes.
Lithograph on tin, 12.5 x 7.2 x 1,8 cm.
Per-megiat (Rus E. Gant) Collection

p. 138, Top to bottom, left to right:
K.K. Tabak-Regie. | 20 Stück | Nil-Cigarretten | Preis per 20St : 1K 20b.
Lithograph on tin, 9.5 x 7.5 x 1.5 cm.
Per-megiat (Rus E. Gant) Collection

Cigarettes.
Harpist, 20 Egyptian cigarettes, manufacturer unknown.
Lithograph on tin, 8.4 x 7.2 x 1.5 cm.
Per-megiat (Rus E. Gant) Collection

Brera | Crüwell-Tabak Siegeszug der ägyptischen Königin Nafretete durch Theben | Gebr. Crüwell Spezialfabrik für Rauchtabak gegr. 1705 Bielefeld.
Brera-Feinschnitt ist von hervorragender Qualitat besonders leicht,
mild und wohlbekommlich, 50 Gramm Ges. Gesh Z.R. No. 417090+494331.
Lithograph on tin, 11 x 8 x 2.5 cm.
Per-megiat (Rus E. Gant) Collection

Egyptian Cigarette and Tobacco Manufactory | Ombos | Cigarette Company | Cairo | (Egypt).
20 Favorite Egyptian Cigarettes.
Lithograph on tin, 9 x 7.2 x 1.8 cm.
Per-megiat (Rus E. Gant) Collection

p. 139, Top to bottom:
Amsterdam London | Egyptian Cigarettes | Hadges Nessim | Purveyor to the Italian Government | Registered Trade Mark | Hadges Nessim, | Alexandria, | Purveyor to | H.R.H. the Khedive.
100 Princess Mansour Cigarettes.
Lithograph on tin, 15.2 x 14.8 x 4 cm.
Per-megiat (Rus E. Gant) Collection

Cleopatra | egyiptomi szivarka | Magyar Királyi Dohányjövedék.
100 Darab 13.50.P Különlegességi Gyártmány.
Lithograph on tin, 13.8 x 10.8 x 3.6 cm.
Per-megiat (Rus E. Gant) Collection

p. 140, Top to bottom:
Manufacture De Cigarettes | Egyptiennes | Luxor | Royale | Continental Cigarette C°. | Salonique-Bruxelles.
20 Cigarettes.
Lithograph on tin, 9.5 x 7.5 x 1.8 cm.
Per-megiat (Rus E. Gant) Collection

Milla | Orient-Auslese | Nach Ägyptischer Art.
24 Cigaretten Milla.
Lithograph on tin, 10 x 7.5 x 2 cm.
Per-megiat (Rus E. Gant) Collection

p. 141, Top to bottom, left to right:
Nebo | Cigarettes | Egyptiennes.
10 Cigarettes, Dans La Fabrication De Ces Cigarettes On Ne Se Sert
Exclusivement Que [De] Meilleures Sortes De Tabac.
Lithograph on tin, 8.5 x 7.2 x 1 cm.
Per-megiat (Rus E. Gant) Collection

Manufacture de Cigarettes Egyptiennes | "Le Khédive" | Ed. Laurens | Alexandrie | & Caire Egypte | Ed. Laurens | Laurens, Bruxelles ... .
Styx Extension Belge.
Lithograph on tin, 13.5 x 10 x 3.5 cm.
Per-megiat (Rus E. Gant) Collection

Murad | The | Turkish |Cigarette |S. Anargyros | Capital Stock Owned By P. Lorillard Co.
100 Egyptian Cigarettes.
Lithograph on tin, 14 x 11 x 3 cm.
Per-megiat (Rus E. Gant) Collection

Manufactory Of The Best | Egyptian Cigarettes | M. Melachrino & C° | "Grands Dépôts" | ... .
London, Cairo, Shanghai, Montreal, Cavalla, Samsoun, Xanthis, Smyrna,
50 No. 9 Egyptian Cigarettes.
Lithograph on tin, 13.7 x 10.5 x 1.5 cm.
Per-megiat (Rus E. Gant) Collection

Cigarettes | Hermes | Mixed.
Egyptian Chapchal Frères Manufacturers Cairo, Egypt.
Cardboard, 6.8 x 5.3 x 2.5 cm.
Per-megiat (Rus E. Gant) Collection

p. 142, Top to bottom, left to right:
African Cigarette | Company L^{td} | Registered Trade Mark | Cairo Egypt | Cairo. Alexandria. Port Said. | Khartoum. London & Bristol.
Cigarette box label, mid 20th century.
Paper, 13.5 x 8.5 cm.
Per-megiat (Rus E. Gant) Collection

Bodourian | Egyptian | Cigarettes | Cairo-Egypt.
Cigarette box label, mid 20th century.
Paper, 9 x 6.2 cm.
Per-megiat (Rus E. Gant) Collection

Freyha | Trade Mark | Pont-Beyrouth (Liban).
Cigarette box label, early 20th century.
Paper, 12.3 x 8.4 cm.
Per-megiat (Rus E. Gant) Collection

Sambul | The Orient Cigarette Coy. | Cairo | 20 Cigarettes "Sambul".
Cigarette box label, early 20th century.
Paper, 10.5 x 7 cm.
Per-megiat (Rus E. Gant) Collection

Anglo-Egyptian |Trade Mark | N°1 | Anglo-Egyptian | Cigarette & Tobacco Co. | London & New York.
Cigarette box label, early 20th century.
Paper, 16 x 7 cm.
Per-megiat (Rus E. Gant) Collection

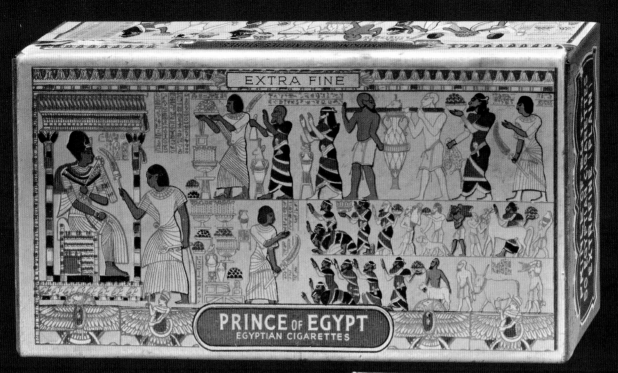

EXTRA FINE

PRINCE OF EGYPT
EGYPTIAN CIGARETTES

Egyptian Cigarette Company
G.M.B.H.
BERLIN - Cairo - BRUSSELS
Egypt

TRADE MARK

AHURI SHU

REGISTERED

HALPAUS
ACLESTO

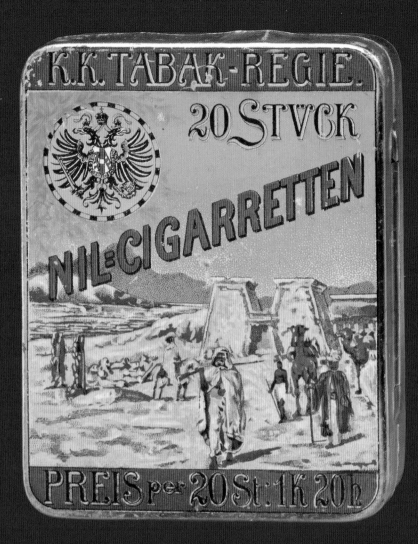

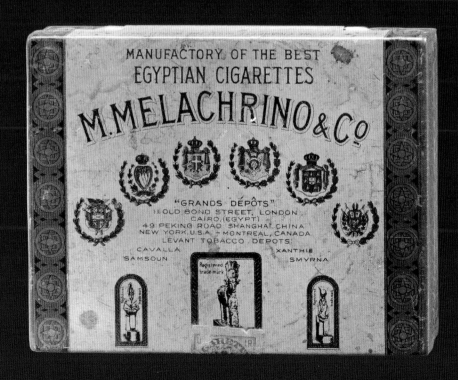

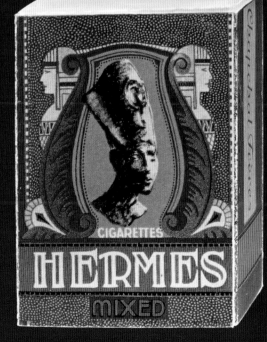

Appendices

Chronological Table

Abydos: The famous List of the Kings

Predynastic Period   c. 5300-3000 BCE

Lower Egypt
Maadi Cultural Complex   c. 4000-3200 BCE

Upper Egypt
Badarian Period   c. 4400-4000 BCE
Amratian (Naqada I) Period   c. 4000-3500 BCE
Gerzean (Naqada II) Period   c. 3500-3200 BCE

After c. 3200 BCE, same chronological sequence for the whole of Egypt

Naqada III/"Dynasty 0"   c. 3200-3000 BCE

Early Dynastic Period   c. 3000-2686 BCE

1st Dynasty   c. 3000-2890
Aha
Djer
Djet
Den
Queen Merneith
Anedjib
Semerkhet
Qa'a

2nd Dynasty   2890-2686
Hetepsekhemwy
Raneb
Nynetjer
Weneg
Sened
Peribsen
Khasekhemwy

Old Kingdom   2686-2160 BCE

3rd Dynasty   2686-2613
Netjerikhet (Djoser)
Sekhemkhet
Khaba
Sanakht Nebka
Huni

4th Dynasty   2613-2494
Sneferu   2613-2589
Khufu (Cheops)   2589-2566
Radjedef   2566-2558
Khafra (Chephren)   2558-2532
Menkaura (Mycerinus)   2532-2503
Shepseskaf   2503-2498

5th Dynasty   2494-2345
Userkaf   2494-2487
Sahura   2487-2475
Neferirkara   2475-2455
Shepseskara   2455-2448
Raneferef   2448-2445
Nyuserra   2445-2421
Menkauhor   2421-2414
Djedkara   2414-2375
Unas   2375-2345

6th Dynasty   2345-2181
Teti   2345-2323
Userkara   2323-2321
Pepy I (Meryra)   2321-2287
Merenra   2287-2278
Pepy II (Neferkara)   2278-2184
Nitiqret   2184-2181

7th and 8th Dynasties   2181-2160
Numerous kings, called Neferkara, in imitation of Pepy II

First Intermediate Period   2160-2055 BCE

9th and 10th Dynasties   2160-2025

11th Dynasty (Thebes only)   2125-2055
Mentuhotep I (Tepy-a: "the ancestor")
Intef I (Sehertawy)   2125-2112
Intef II (Wahankh)   2112-2063
Intef III (Nakhtnebtepnefer)   2063-2055

Middle Kingdom   2055-1650 BCE

11th Dynasty (all Egypt)   2055-1985
Mentuhotep II (Nebhepetra)   2055-2004
Mentuhotep III (Sankhkara)   2004-1992
Mentuhotep IV (Nebtawyra)   1992-1985

12th Dynasty   1985-1773
Amenemhat I (Sehetepibra)   1985-1956
Senuseret I (Kheperkara)   1956-1911
Amenemhat II (Nubkaura)   1911-1877
Senuseret II (Khakheperra)   1877-1870
Senuseret III (Khakaura)   1870-1831
Amenemhat III (Nimaatra)   1831-1786
Amenemhat IV (Maakherura)   1786-1777
Queen Sobekneferu (Sobekkara)   1777-1773

13th Dynasty   1773-after 1650
Wegaf (Khutawyra)
Sobekhotep II (Sekhemra-khutawy)
Iykhernefert Neferhotep (Sankhtawy-sekhemra)
Ameny-intef-amenemhat (Sankhibra)
Hor (Awibra)
Khendjer (Userkara)
Sobekhotep III (Sekhemra-sewadjtawy)
Neferhotep I (Khasekhemra)
Sahathor
Sobekhotep IV (Khaneferra)
Sobekhotep V
Ay (Merneferra)

14th Dynasty   1773-1650
Minor rulers probably contemporary with the 13th or 15th Dynasty

Second Intermediate Period   1650-1550 BCE

15th Dynasty (Hyksos)   1650-1550

16th Dynasty   1650-1580
Theban early rulers contemporary with the 15th Dynasty

17th Dynasty   c. 1580-1550
Rahotep
Sobekemsaf I
Intef VI (Sekhemra)
Intef VII (Nubkheperra)
Intef VIII (Sekhemraherhermaat)
Sobekemsaf II
Siamun (?)
Taa (Senakhtenra/Seqenenra)   c. 1560
Kamose (Wadjkheperra)   1555-1550

New Kingdom   1550-1069 BCE

18th Dynasty   1550-1295
Ahmose (Nebpehtyra)   1550-1525
Amenhotep I (Djeserkara)   1525-1504
Thutmose I (Aakheperkara)   1504-1492
Thutmose II (Aakheperenra)   1492-1479
Thutmose III (Menkheperra)   1479-1425
Queen Hatshepsut (Maatkara)   1473-1458
Amenhotep II (Aakheperura)   1427-1400
Thutmose IV (Menkheperura)   1400-1390
Amenhotep III (Nebmaatra)   1390-1352
Amenhotep IV/Akhenaten (Neferkheperurawaenra)   1352-1336

Neferneferuaten (Smenkhkara)	1338-1336
Tutankhamun (Nebkheperura)	1336-1327
Ay (Kheperkheperura)	1327-1323
Horemheb (Djeserkheperura)	1323-1295

Ramessid Period
1295-1069 BCE

19ᵗʰ Dynasty	1295-1186
Ramesses I (Menpehtyra)	1295-1294
Sety I (Menmaatra)	1294-1279
Ramesses II (Usermaatra Setepenra)	1279-1213
Merenptah (Baenra)	1213-1203
Amenmessu (Menmira)	1203-1200?
Sety II (Userkheperura Setepenra)	1200-1194
Siptah (Akhenrasetepenra)	1194-1188
Queen Tausret (Sitrameritamun)	1188-1186
20ᵗʰ Dynasty	1186-1069
Sethnakht (Userkhaura Meryamun)	1186-1184
Ramesses III (Usermaatra Meryamun)	1184-1153
Ramesses IV (Heqamaatra Setepenamun)	1153-1147
Ramesses V (Usermaatra Sekheperenra)	1147-1143
Ramesses VI (Nebmaatra Meryamun)	1143-1136
Ramesses VII (Usermaatra Setepenra Meryamun)	1136-1129
Ramesses VIII (Usermaatra Akhenamun)	1129-1126
Ramesses IX (Neferkara Setepenra)	1126-1108
Ramesses X (Khepermaatra Setepenra)	1108-1099
Ramesses XI (Menmaatra Setepenptah)	1099-1069

Third Intermediate Period
1069-664 BCE

21ˢᵗ Dynasty	1069-945
Smendes (Hedjkheperra Setepenra)	1069-1043
Amenemnisu (Neferkara)	1043-1039
Psusennes I [Pasebakhaenniut] (Akheperra Setepenamun)	1039-991
Amenemope (Usermaatra Setepenamun)	993-984
Osorkon the Elder (Akheperra Setepenra)	984-978
Siamun (Netjerkheperra Setepenamun)	978-959
Psusennes II [Pasebakhaenniut] (Titkheperura Setepenra)	959-945
22ⁿᵈ Dynasty	945-715
Sheshonq I (Hedjkheperra)	945-924
Osorkon I (Sekhemkheperra)	924-889
Sheshonq II (Heqakheperra)	c. 890
Takelot I	889-874
Osorkon II (Usermaatra)	874-850
Takelot II (Hedjkheperra)	850-825
Sheshonq III (Usermaatra)	825-773
Pimay (Usermaatra)	773-767
Sheshonq V (Aakheperra)	767-730
Osorkon IV (Aakheperra)	730-715
23ʳᵈ Dynasty	818-715
Kings in various centres, contemporary with the later 22ⁿᵈ, 24ᵗʰ, and early 25ᵗʰ dynasties	
24ᵗʰ Dynasty	727-715
Bakenrenef (Bocchoris)	720-715
25ᵗʰ Dynasty	747-656
Piy (Menkheperra)	747-716
Shabaqo (Neferkara)	716-702
Shabitqo (Djedkaura)	702-690
Taharqo (Khunefertemra)	690-664
Tanutamani (Bakara)	664-656

Late Period
664-332 BCE

26ᵗʰ Dynasty	664-525
[Nekau I	672-664]
Psamtek I (Wahibra)	664-610
Nekau II (Wehemibra)	610-595
Psamtek II (Neferibra)	595-589
Apries (Haaibra)	589-570
Ahmose II [Amasis] (Khnemibra)	570-526
Psamtek III (Ankhkaenra)	526-525
27ᵗʰ Dynasty (1ˢᵗ Persian Period)	525-404
Cambyses	525-522
Darius I	522-486
Xerxes I	486-465
Artaxerxes I	465-424
Darius II	424-405
Artaxerxes II	405-359
28ᵗʰ Dynasty	404-399
Amyrtaios	404-399
29ᵗʰ Dynasty	399-380
Nepherites I [Nefaarud]	399-393
Hakor [Achoris] (Khnemmaatra)	393-380
Nepherites II	c. 380
30ᵗʰ Dynasty	380-343
Nectanebo I (Kheperkara)	380-362
Teos (Irma Atenra)	362-360
Nectanebo II (Senedjemibra Setepenanhur)	360-343
2ⁿᵈ Persian Period	343-332
Artaxerxes III Ochus	343-338
Arses	338-336
Darius III Codoman	336-332

Ptolemaic Period
332-30 BCE

Macedonian Dynasty	332-305
Alexander the Great	332-323
Philip Arrhidaeus	323-317
Alexander IV	317-310
Ptolemaic Dynasty	
Ptolemy I Soter I	305-285
Ptolemy II Philadelphus	285-246
Ptolemy III Euergetes I	246-221
Ptolemy IV Philopator	221-205
Ptolemy V Epiphanes	205-180
Ptolemy VI Philometor	180-145
Ptolemy VII Neos Philopator	145
Ptolemy VIII Euergetes II	170-116
Ptolemy IX Soter II	116-107
Ptolemy X Alexander I	107-88
Ptolemy IX Soter II (restored)	88-80
Ptolemy XI Alexander II	80
Ptolemy XII Neos Dionysos (Auletes)	80-51
Cleopatra VII Philopator	51-30
Ptolemy XIII	51-47
Ptolemy XIV	47-44
Ptolemy XV Caesarion	44-30

Roman Period
30 BCE-AD 395

Bizantin Period
395-639

Arab Conquest
639-641

The present chronology is mostly based on
I. SHAW, *The Oxford History of Ancient Egypt*, Oxford 2000, pp. 479-483.

148

Egyptological Archives and Library of the Università degli Studi di Milano. Bibliography (1999-2011)

Christian Orsenigo

I. *Books and articles*
using, studying or describing documents kept in the Egyptological Archives and Library

1999

P. Piacentini, "L'antico Egitto a Milano in una biblioteca straordinaria", in *Ca' de Sass* 145 (1999), pp. 28, 30-35.

G. Pontiggia, "Aura arcana e durevoli suggestioni", in *Ca' de Sass* 145 (1999), p. 29.

[E.W. Seibel], *The Egyptological Library of Elmar Edel*, Ars Libri, Boston 1999.

2000

P. Piacentini, "A Milano la Biblioteca di Egittologia di Elmar Edel", in *Sistema Università*, anno V, n. 1 (gennaio/febbraio 2000), pp. 12-13.

P. Piacentini, "Dalla riscoperta dell'Egitto all'Egittologia. La sezione egittologica della biblioteca del Dipartimento di Scienze dell'Antichità dell'Università degli Studi di Milano, in *Acme* 53/3 (2000), pp. 201-210, figs 1-6.

P. Piacentini, *L'Antico Egitto di Napoleone*, Milano 2000.
Reviews:
F. Tiradritti, "L'Egitto perduto di Napoleone", in *Il Giornale dell'Arte*, anno XVIII, n. 196 (febbraio 2001), p. 62.
Archeologia Viva, anno XX, n. 86 (marzo/aprile 2001), p. 110.

P. Piacentini, "Una nuova acquisizione dell'Università degli Studi di Milano: gli autografi e la biblioteca di Elmar Edel", in S. Russo (ed.), *Atti del V Convegno Nazionale di Egittologia e Papirologia, Firenze, 10-12 dicembre 1999*, Firenze 2000, pp. 185-189.

2001

P. Piacentini, "Victor Loret et les scribes de Saqqara", in *GRAFMA* 5/6 (2001-2002), pp. 54-69.

[E.W. Seibel], *Egyptology. The Library of Alexandre Varille*, Ars Libri, Boston 2001.

2002

P. Piacentini, *La Biblioteca e gli Archivi di Egittologia del Dipartimento di Scienze dell'Antichità dell'Università degli Studi di Milano* (Catalogue of the exhibition), Novara 2002.

P. Piacentini, M. Pozzi Battaglia (eds), *Egitto. Dalle piramidi ad Alessandro Magno* (Catalogue of the exhibition), Milano 2002.

P. Piacentini, V. Rondot, "1881, Musée de Boulaq, mort de Mariette", in M. Eldamaty, M. Trad (eds), *Egyptian Museum Collections around the World. Studies for the Centennial of the Egyptian Museum, Cairo*, II, Cairo 2002, pp. 949-956.

P. Piacentini, E.W. Seibel, "L'egittologo bibliofilo", in P. Piacentini, M. Pozzi Battaglia (eds), *Egitto. Dalle piramidi ad Alessandro Magno* (Catalogue of the exhibition), Milano 2002, pp. 17-21.

2003

M.E. Peroschi, "Breve storia della Biblioteca di Egittologia presso l'Università di Milano (parte prima)", in *Associazione donne italiane al Cairo* (marzo/aprile 2003), pp. 8-9.

M.E. Peroschi, "Breve storia, in due puntate, della Biblioteca di Egittologia del Dipartimento di Scienze dell'Antichità dell'Università degli Studi di Milano (parte seconda)", in *Associazione donne italiane al Cairo* (maggio 2003), pp. 8-9.

P. Piacentini, "La biblioteca di Alexandre Varille e le prime fotografie aeree dell'Egitto", in C. Basile, A. Di Natale (eds), *Atti del VII Convegno nazionale di Egittologia e Papirologia, Siracusa, 29 novembre - 2 dicembre 2001* (Quaderni del Museo del Papiro 2), Siracusa 2003, pp. 133-143.

P. Piacentini, "L'Egitto in mostra a Milano. Libri e archivi", in *L'Erasmo. Bimestrale della civiltà europea* 13 (gennaio/febbraio 2003), pp. 101-103.

P. Piacentini, "'Wonderful things' on paper. The Egyptologist Victor Loret in the Valley of the Kings", in *Apollo. The International Magazine of the Arts* (July 2003), pp. 3-8.

G. Quattrocchi, "Dalle piramidi ad Alessandro Magno. Tre millenni di storia egiziana in mostra a Milano", in *Archeo*, anno XIX, n. 2 (febbraio 2003), pp. 16-17.

2004

AA.VV., *Egitto. Dalle piramidi ad Alessandro Magno: guida alla mostra* (Catalogue of the exhibition), Cremona 2004.

L. Gordan-Rastelli, "Egypt & Egyptology in Cremona, Italy as showcased in the exhibition 'Egypt: From the Pyramids to Alexander the Great'", in *KMT. A Modern Journal of Ancient Egypt*, vol. 15, n. 4 (Winter 2004-2005), pp. 45-53.

P. Piacentini, "La Biblioteca e gli Archivi di Egittologia", in A. Negri, M. Valsecchi (eds), *Il tesoro della Statale. Collezioni e identità di un grande Ateneo* (Catalogue of the exhibition), Milano 2004, pp. 52-59, 64, 121.

P. Piacentini, "La Biblioteca e gli Archivi di Egittologia. Nuove acquisizioni e attività in corso", in V. de Angelis (ed.), *Sviluppi recenti nell'antichistica. Nuovi contributi* (Quaderni di Acme 68), Milano 2004, pp. 109-125, pls 11-13.

P. Piacentini, "Saqqarah, 15 août 1897 - 12 février 1899. Les journaux de fouilles et autres documents inédits de Victor Loret", in *Aegyptus*, anno LXXXIV (2004), pp. 3-20.

P. Piacentini, C. Orsenigo, *La Valle dei Re riscoperta. I giornali di scavo di Victor Loret (1898-1899) e altri inediti* (Le vetrine del sapere 1), Milano 2004 [English translation by S. Quirke, *The Valley of the Kings rediscovered. The Victor Loret excavation journals (1898-1899) and other manuscripts*, Milano 2005].
Reviews:
S. Einaudi, in *Il Giornale dell'Arte*, anno XXIII, n. 243 (maggio 2005), p. 61.
D.C. Forbes, in KMT. *A Modern Journal of Ancient Egypt*, vol. 16, n. 3 (Fall 2005), p. 87.
R.B. Partridge, in *Ancient Egypt. The History, People and Culture of the Nile Valley*, vol. 6, n. 3, issue 33 (December 2005/January 2006), pp. 59-60.
P. Vernus, in *Aegyptus*, anno LXXXIII (gennaio/dicembre 2003), pp. 300-305.
Archeo, anno XXI, n. 8 (agosto 2005).
Archeologia Viva, anno XXIV, n. 113 (settembre/ottobre 2005), pp. 82-83.

2005

P. Piacentini, "La deuxième cachette royale revisitée d'après les notes de Victor Loret", in *Égypte Afrique & Orient* 38 (juin 2005), pp. 57-66.

P. Piacentini, C. Orsenigo, "Loret's Unknown Activities in the Valley of the Kings (1898-1899): From the Surveys to the Second Royal Cache", in *The 56th Annual Meeting of the American Research Center in Egypt, April 22-24, 2005, Cambridge, MA* (abstracts of papers), Atlanta 2005, pp. 83-84.

P. Piacentini, C. Orsenigo, "Nella Valle dei Re", in *Sistema Università*, anno IV, n. 12 (giugno 2005), pp. 3-4.

2006

C. Orsenigo, "Il visir e la proclamazione dei giubilei in epoca Ramesside", in C. Mora, P. Piacentini (eds), *L'Ufficio e il Documento. I luoghi, i modi, gli strumenti dell'amministrazione in Egitto e nel Vicino Oriente antico* (Quaderni di Acme 83), Milano 2006, pp. 109-118.

P. Piacentini (ed.), *Gli archivi egittologici dell'Università degli Sudi di Milano. 1. Il fondo Elmar Edel* (Il Filarete 230), Milano 2006.
Reviews:
M. Patanè, in *BiOr* 64 (2007), pp. 611-612.
G. Poethke, in *AfP* 53/1 (2007), pp. 71-72.
A. Roccati, in *Archaeogate. Il Portale Italiano di Archeologia* (8 novembre 2006), available at http://www.archaeogate.org/egittologia/pubblicazi one/333/patrizia-piacentini-a-cura-di-gli-archivi-egittologici.html
CdÉ 82 (2007), p. 200.

P. Piacentini, C. Orsenigo, "I taccuini perduti", in *Pharaon Magazine*, anno II, n. 1 (gennaio 2006), pp. 80-87.

2007

A. Gasse, V. Rondot, *Les inscriptions de Séhel* (MIFAO 126), Le Caire 2007.

C. Orsenigo, "La découverte du tombeau de Maiherperi (KV 36) dans les notes inédites de Victor Loret, in J.-C. Goyon, C. Cardin (eds), *Proceedings of the Ninth International Congress of Egyptologists / Actes du neuvième Congrès international des Égyptologues Grenoble, 6-12 septembre 2004* (OLA 150/2), Leuven - Paris - Dudley, MA 2007, pp. 1429-1436.

C. Orsenigo, "Victor Loret e Félix Guilmant nella tomba di Ramesse IX", in G. Zanetto, S. Martinelli Tempesta, M. Ornaghi (eds), *Vestigia Antiquitatis* (Quaderni di Acme 89), Milano 2007, pp. 229-237.

P. Piacentini, "De Mariette à Edel: Les archives égyptologiques de l'Université de Milan", in J.-C. Goyon, C. Cardin (eds), *Proceedings of the Ninth International Congress of Egyptologists / Actes du neuvième Congrès international des Égyptologues Grenoble, 6-12 septembre 2004* (OLA 150/2), Leuven - Paris - Dudley, MA 2007, pp. 1509-1518.

P. Piacentini, "Victor Loret et la tombe d'Aménophis II", in *Les grandes civilisations. L'Égypte pharaonique* (Le Point hors-série), Paris nov-déc. 2007, pp. 124-125.

P. Piacentini, "William Kelly Simpson dona il suo epistolario agli Archivi egittologici dell'Università degli Studi di Milano", in *Archaeogate. Il Portale Italiano di Archeologia* (31 maggio 2007), available at http://www.archaeogate.org/egittologia/article/588/1/

P. Piacentini, "William Kelly Simpson: una pagina di egittologia e di storia americana a Milano", in *Sistema Università*, anno V, n. 21 (settembre 2007), pp. 8-9.

P. Piacentini, G. Mantegari, "A Project for the Management and Publication of University of Milan's Egyptological Archives", in J.T. Clark, E.M. Hagemeister (eds), *Digital Discovery: Exploring New Frontiers in Human Heritage, 34th Conference on Computer Applications and Quantitative Methods in Archaeology, Fargo, ND-USA, 18-23 April, 2006. Proceedings*, Budapest 2007, pp. 382-389.

2008

P. Cosmacini, P. Piacentini, "L'Egitto ai raggi X", in *Archeo*, anno XXIV, n. 11 (novembre 2008), pp. 71-75.

P. Cosmacini, P. Piacentini, "Notes on the history of the radiological study of Egyptian mummies: from x-rays to new imaging techniques / Appunti sulla storia dello studio radiografico delle mummie anticoegiziane: dalla radiografia convenzionale alle più recenti tecniche di immagine", in *La radiologia medica. Official Journal of the Italian Society of Medical Radiology*, vol. 113, n. 5 (August 2008), pp. 615-626.

A. Ferri (ed.), with contributions by C. Busi, P. Piacentini, I. Zannier, L. Marucchi, *Il Fotografo dei Faraoni. Antonio Beato in Egitto 1860-1905* (Obiettivi sul passato 1) (Catalogue of the exhibition), Bologna 2008 [with English translation].

F. Janot, with introduction by Z. Hawass, *The Royal Mummies: Immortality in Ancient Egypt*, Cairo 2008.

M. Marra, *R.A. Schwaller de Lubicz. La politica, l'esoterismo, l'egittologia* (I Libri di Airesis 1), Milano 2008.

C. Orsenigo, "Alexandre Varille e la stele di Ramessemperra del Museo di Vienne", in G. Zanetto, S. Martinelli Tempesta, M. Ornaghi (eds), *Nova Vestigia Antiquitatis* (Quaderni di Acme 102), Milano 2008, pp. 195-207.

C. Orsenigo, "Kings' Valley Tomb 37: analysis of finds from Loret's 1899 excavations", in *GM* 216 (2008), pp. 61-74.

P. Piacentini, *Gli archivi egittologici in mostra al Cairo*, in *Sistema Università*, anno VI, n. 26 (dicembre 2008), pp. 8-9.

P. Piacentini (ed.), with contributions by Z. Hawass, W. El-Saddik, E.W. Seibel, P. Piacentini, L. Pantalacci, C. Orsenigo, *Victor Loret in Egypt (1881-1899). From the Archives of the Milan University to the Egyptian Museum in Cairo* (Catalogue of the exhibition), Cairo 2008 [Arabic translation by T. El-Awady, Cairo 2008].

2009

A. Ferri (ed.), with contributions by C. Busi, P. Piacentini, I. Zannier, L. Marucchi, *Il Fotografo dei Faraoni. Antonio Beato in Egitto 1860-1905* (Catalogue of the exhibition), Cairo 2009 [with English and Arabic translation].

P. Piacentini, "Auguste Mariette in the Egyptological Archives and Library of the University of Milan", in D. Magee, J. Bourriau, S. Quirke (eds), *Sitting Beside Lepsius. Studies in Honour of Jaromir Malek at the Griffith Institute* (OLA 185), Leiden 2009, pp. 423-438.

P. Piacentini, "Editorial. Ten Years Later", in *EDAL* 1 (2009), pp. 11-20, pls I-IX.

P. Piacentini, C. Orsenigo, "The discovery of the tomb of Mose and its 'juridical' inscription", in *Iid.* (eds), *Egyptian Archives. Proceedings of the First Session of the International Congress Egyptian Archives / Egyptological Archives, Milano, September 9-10, 2008* (Quaderni di Acme 111), Milano 2009, pp. 83-102.

2010

P. Cosmacini, P. Piacentini, C. Orsenigo, D. Lauretti, M. Sabato, G. Fornaciari, *Studio radiografico delle mummie antico egiziane dalla prima "lastra" all'immagine 3D* (poster presented at the *44° Congresso Nazionale SIRM* (*Società Italiana di Radiografia Medica*), Verona, 11-15 giugno 2010.

P. Marangoni, P. Piacentini *et al.*, *Kofler. Cairo 1914* (I Quaderni della Stanza), Bolzano 2010.

P. Piacentini, "Archaeology and Archives: the Egyptian Museums in Egypt at the End of the Nineteenth Century", in F. Raffaele, M. Nuzzolo, I. Incordino (eds), *Recent Discoveries and Latest Researches in Egyptology: Proceedings of the First Neapolitan Congress of Egyptology, Neaples June 18th-20th 2008*, Wiesbaden 2010, pp. 221-236.

P. Piacentini, "Dalla ricerca archeologica agli archivi: studi sulle tombe tebane tra la West Bank e Milano", in *RISE* 4 (2010), pp. 301-319.

P. Piacentini, "Dall'Ezbekieh a Piazza Tahrir. Breve storia del Museo Egizio del Cairo", in *Ead.*, G. Pinna (eds), *Museologia egiziana* (Nuova Museologia 23), Milano 2010, pp. 14-21.

P. Piacentini (ed.). *Egypt and the Pharaohs. From the Sand to the Library. Pharaonic Egypt in the Archives and Libraries of the Università degli Studi di Milano* (Le vetrine del sapere 9), Ginevra - Milano 2010.

P. Piacentini, "I musei egiziani e l'Università degli Studi di Milano: attività di collaborazione e ricerche d'archivio", in G. Zanetto, M. Ornaghi (eds), *Documenta Antiquitatis* (Quaderni di Acme 120), Milano 2010, pp. 171-202.

P. Piacentini, "Percorsi dell'Egittologia all'inizio del XIX secolo: musei e tutela delle collezioni", in M.B. Failla, C. Piva (eds), *L'"arte senza imitazione". Musei e collezioni di antichità egizie all'epoca di Champollion* (Ricerche di Storia dell'Arte 100), Roma 2010, pp. 13-21.

II. *News and articles on newspapers and magazines* on the activities of the Egyptological Archives and Library (new acquisitions, exhibitions and publications)[1]

"Alla Statale per 2 miliardi una biblioteca sull'Egitto", in *Il Giornale* (30 novembre 1999).

"L'Egitto in una biblioteca", in *Avvenire* (30 novembre 1999).

G. Locati, "L'Egitto a Milano in 10mila volumi", in *Il Giornale* (1 dicembre 1999).

A. Malnati, "Finalmente a Milano un tesoro d'Egitto", in *Il Giorno* (1 dicembre 1999).

P. Panza, "Milano batte New York e diventa capitale dell'Egittologia", in *Corriere della Sera* (1 dicembre 1999).

"I misteri d'Egitto in 10mila volumi", in *La Repubblica* (1 dicembre 1999).

"Biblía la memoria del futuro", suppl. a *L'altra enigmistica*, anno XXV, n. 5 (maggio 2001).

"La biblioteca Edel", in *Sistema Università*, anno VI, n. 10 (dicembre 2001), p. 9.

P. Piacentini, "Nuova biblioteca di Egittologia", in *Archeologia Viva*, anno XXI, n. 92 (marzo/aprile 2002), p. 9.

A. Malnati, "La Statale come Alessandria d'Egitto", in *Il Giornale* (5 maggio 2002).

C. Brambilla, "L'egittologa nella Rete", in *La Repubblica* (8 maggio 2002).

R. Uboldi, "Cleopatra abita a Milano", in *Il Tempo* (9 maggio 2002).

P. Panza, "E adesso alla Statale si iscrivono anche i faraoni", in *Corriere della Sera* (13 maggio 2002).

"Milano Statale, la nuova piramide del sapere", in *Campus web* (maggio 2002).

"Egittologia. Apre a Milano la nuova Biblioteca", in *Quark* (2 giugno 2002).

G. degli Agosti, "Libri, documenti e fotografie testimoniano il cammino nella terra dei faraoni dai primi scavi all'archeologia scientifica", in *L'Osservatore Romano* (14 giugno 2002).

"I segreti delle piramidi sono a Milano", in *La Macchina del Tempo*, anno III, n. 7 (luglio 2002), p. 47.

"La biblioteca di Egittologia del Dipartimento di Scienze dell'Antichità", in *Informazione Universitaria*, anno VIII, n. 2 (luglio 2002), p. 11.

D.C. Forbes, "Editor's Report", in *KMT. A Modern Journal of Ancient Egypt*, vol. 13, n. 2 (Summer 2002), p. 2 [on the acquisition of the Varille Archives].

---

1. The Egyptological Archives and Library of the Università degli Studi di Milano have been often mentioned in websites: we have chosen to list here only the most important articles appeared on the Web. We have also omitted the TV and radio programs during which the Archives and Library have been mentioned or shown, and the lectures on the subject.

[M.H. Trindade Lopes], "Inauguração da Biblioteca de Egiptologia da Universidade de Milão", in *Hathor: estudos de egiptologia* 5 (2002), p. 150.

G. Pittiglio, "L'Egitto in biblioteca", in *Galileo. Giornale di scienza e problemi globali* (27 gennaio 2003), available on the web.

"Abstractio mors", in *Sistema Università*, anno III, n. 9 (settembre 2004), p. 8.

"A Cremona i segreti dell'Antico Egitto", in *Il Sole 24 Ore* (1 ottobre 2004).

"Il segreto dell'egittologo", in *Il Giornale di Brescia* (27 ottobre 2004).

A. Massolini, "I segreti dell'Egitto svelati in Valsabbia", in *Bresciaoggi* (8 novembre 2004).

"La Valle dei Re riscoperta: un nuovo volume per la Collana di Ateneo", in *Sistema Università*, anno III, n. 10 (dicembre 2004), p. 10.

P. Panza, "Il mistero dell'antico Egitto, alla Statale la Valle dei Re", in *Corriere della Sera* (11 marzo 2005).

A. Malnati, "Gli scavi eroici di Loret, Indiana Jones dell'Ottocento", in *Il Giorno - Ed. Metropoli* (13 marzo 2005).

"La riscoperta della Valle dei Re", in *La Repubblica* (13 marzo 2005).

"L'egittologo Loret", in *Avvenire* (13 marzo 2005).

"La Valle dei Re riscoperta", in *City - Ed. Milano* (14 marzo 2005).

M. Tedoldi, "'La Valle dei re riscoperta' grazie ai documenti di scavo ritrovati dall'Università di Milano, in *Il Giornale di Brescia* (21 marzo 2005).

I. Paolucci, "Victor Loret, che Grande Passione l'Egitto", in *L'Unità* (3 aprile 2005).

"La Valle dei Re riscoperta con gli appunti dell'egittologo", in *La Gazzetta del Mezzogiorno* (3 aprile 2005).

I. Principe, "Egitto, la Statale ripubblica 'I giornali di scavo' di Loret", in *Il Giornale* (10 aprile 2005).

"Riscoperta la Valle dei Re", in *La Provincia. Quotidiano di Cremona e Crema* (15 aprile 2005).

G. degli Agosti, "I tesori della Valle dei Re rivivono nei 'giornali di scavo' di Victor Loret", in *L'Osservatore Romano* (2 luglio 2005).

D. Moyer, "For the Record", in *KMT. A Modern Journal of Ancient Egypt*, vol. 16, n. 3 (Fall 2005), p. 10 [on the volume *La Valle dei Re riscoperta*].

G. Boulad, "La Vallée des rois redécouverte", in *Al-Ahram Hebdo en ligne* 615 (21-27 juin 2006), available at http://hebdo.ahram.org.eg/arab/ahram/2006/6/21/voy1.htm

"Egyptology", in *Special Bullettin ars libri* 113 (December 2006), [unnumbered page].

M. Mariani, "L'Antico Egitto da sognare e da capire", in *Università aperta terza pagina*, anno XVII, n. 5 (maggio 2007), p. 17.

A. Malnati, "L'Egitto dall'America. La collezione Simpson donata alla Statale", in *Avvenire* (5 giugno 2007).

A. Malnati, "Una biblioteca tematica tra le più fornite al mondo", in *Avvenire* (5 giugno 2007).

"Upcoming Events", in *The Egyptian Museum Newsletter* 1 (January/April 2008), p. [2] [on the exhibition *Victor Loret in Egypt*].

C.T. de Vartavan, "Our predecessors in the study of 'The Plants of Ancient Egypt': Victor Loret (1859-1946)", in *Armenian Egyptology Centre Newsletter*, vol. 1, issue 3 (1 May 2008), p. 3, available at http://aegyptology.atspace.com/AEC3/index_files/Page360.htm

"Temporary Exhibition: Victor Loret in Egypt (1881-1899). From the Archives of the Milan University to the Egyptian Museum in Cairo", in *The Egyptian Museum Newsletter* 2 (May/August 2008), p. [2].

[A. Navarro], "Le pionnier français Victor Loret de retour en Égypte pour livrer ses secrets" (11 juin 2008), available on the web.

R.B. Partridge, "If you are visiting Cairo shortly ...", in *Ancient Egypt. The History, People and Culture of the Nile Valley*, vol. 8, n. 6, issue 48 (June/July 2008), p. 7 [on the exhibition *Victor Loret in Egypt*].

P. Panza, "Tesoro von Bothmer: l'Università Statale diventa capitale degli Archivi egizi", in *Corriere della Sera* (9 settembre 2008).

S. Ikram, "Nile currents", in *KMT. A Modern Journal of Ancient Egypt*, vol. 19, n. 3 (Fall 2008), p. 8 [on the exhibition *Victor Loret in Egypt*].

"Exhibitions", in *The Egyptian Museum Newsletter* 3 (September/December 2008), p. [2] [on the exhibition *Victor Loret in Egypt*].

A. Wahby Taher, "The Victor Loret Exhibition at the Egyptian Museum in Cairo", in *Ancient Egypt. The History, People and Culture of the Nile Valley*, vol. 9, n. 2, issue 50 (October/November 2008), pp. 13-14.

"Museo egipcio de El Cairo abre exposición sobre su historia y antecedents", in *Terra Actualidad* (19 Octubre 2008), available at http://terranoticias.terra.es/cultura/articulo/museo-egipcio-cairo-2826913.htm

N. El-Aref, "The GEM of history", in *Al-Ahram Weekly On-line*, n. 920 (30 October-5 November 2008), available at http://weekly.ahram.org.eg/2008/920/he1.htm

D. Elhami, "Du Tibre au Nil, coopération tous azimuts", in *Al-Ahram Hebdo en ligne*, n. 739 (5-11 novembre 2008), available on the web.

S. Ikram, "Nile currents", in *KMT. A Modern Journal of Ancient Egypt*, vol. 19, n. 4 (Winter 2008-2009), p. 5 [on the exhibition *The History of the Egyptian Museum*].

S. Ikram, "Nile currents", in *KMT. A Modern Journal of Ancient Egypt*, vol. 20, n. 1 (Spring 2009), p. 5 [on the exhibition *The History of the Egyptian Museum*].

F. Manzoni, "Violetta de Angelis, l'amica' di Petrarca e Dante", in *Corriere della Sera* (16 febbraio 2010) [on Professor de Angelis' untiring support of the acquisition of the Edel Library].

"'Kofler. Cairo 1914' - Ausstellung zeigt unveröffentlichte Fotos eines unbekannten Fotografen", in *Südtirol Online* (22. Oktober 2010), available at http://www.stol.it/Artikel/Kultur-im-Ueberblick/Kunst/Kofler.-Cairo-1914-Ausstellung-zeigt-unveroeffentlichte-Fotos-eines-unbekannten-Fotografen

C. Pantozzi, "Una mostra al circolo La Stanza cerca di far luce sulle origini altoatesine del fotografo Kofler, un talento dalle origini misteriose", in *Corriere della Sera* - inserto *Alto Adige* (23 ottobre 2010), p. 13.

M. Rizza, "Kofler, il sudtirolese avvolto nel mistero che per primo fotografò l'Egitto. Esposti all'Espace La Stanza otto scatti del 1914, tutti inediti. Ricerca dell'Università di Milano", in *Alto Adige* (23 ottobre 2010), p. 38.

"Wer ist ‚Kofler Cairo 1914?", in *Dolomiten* (23./24. Oktober 2010), pp. 6-7.

S. Smee, "Turning the Page. Ars Libri, a valued destination for art books in Boston, is heading for a new home", in *Boston Sunday Globe - Arts* (March 27, 2011), pp. 1, 6-7 [on the discovery of the Varille/Loret Archives and their acquisition by the University of Milan, on p. 7].

III. *Thesis on documents*
preserved in the Egyptological
Archives and Library carried out
under the supervision
of Prof. Patrizia Piacentini

Bachelor Degree
(Laurea triennale)

*Digitalizzazione e studio delle lastre fotografiche
degli archivi di Egittologia dell'Università
degli Studi di Milano (siti di Nag'el-Madamud,
Karnak e altri)* (a.a. 2003-2004).

*La corrispondenza tra Alexandre Varille
e gli egittologi di lingua inglese* (a.a. 2003-2004).

*Studio per la catalogazione degli archivi
fotografici A. Varille conservati presso
la Biblioteca e gli Archivi di Egittologia
dell'Università degli Studi di Milano*
(a.a. 2003-2004).

*L'epistolario di Alexandre Varille con egittologi
di lingua francese* (a.a. 2004-2005).

*L'epistolario di Alexandre Varille con egittologi
di lingua francese (1930-1934)* (a.a. 2004-2005).

*Studio e implementazione di un'architettura
per la realizzazione di un sistema software
per l'accesso all'archivio della Biblioteca
di Egittologia dell'Università degli Studi di Milano*
(a.a. 2004-2005. Under the supervision of
Prof. Stefania Bandini and Dr Glauco Mantegari).

*Il sito di El Kab attraverso lo studio di fotografie
dell'archivio Varille dell'Università degli Studi
di Milano* (a.a. 2005-2006).

*Digitalizzazione e studio degli Archivi Egittologici
di A. Varille dell'Università degli Studi di Milano
(Karnak nord)* (a.a. 2006-2007).

*Digitalizzazione e studio degli Archivi Egittologici
di A. Varille dell'Università degli Studi di Milano
(Karnak nord)* (a.a. 2006-2007).

*Il santuario di Heqaib a Elefantina: analisi
delle fotografie del fondo Varille, Archivi
Egittologici dell'Università degli Studi di Milano*
(a.a. 2006-2007).

*Il tempio di Montu a Medamud: analisi del fondo
Varille, Archivi Egittologici dell'Università
degli Studi di Milano* (a.a. 2006-2007).

*L'area archeologica di Karnak nord: analisi
delle fotografie del fondo Varille, Archivi
Egittologici dell'Università degli Studi di Milano*
(a.a. 2006-2007).

*La tomba di Ramose (TT55): analisi
delle fotografie del fondo Varille, Archivi
Egittologici dell'Università degli Studi di Milano*
(a.a. 2006-2007).

*Ricerche sulla Tomba Tebana TT78 di Horemhab:
analisi delle fotografie del fondo Varille,
Archivi Egittologici dell'Università degli Studi
di Milano* (a.a. 2007-2008).

Ricerche sulla Tomba Tebana 181
(a.a. 2007-2008).

Ricerche sulla Tomba Tebana 192
(a.a. 2007-2008).

Ricerche sulle Tombe Tebane TT90 e TT96
(a.a. 2007-2008).

Ricerche sulle Tombe Tebane TT161 e TT178
(a.a. 2007-2008).

Ricerche sulle Tombe Tebane 253 e 295
(a.a. 2007-2008).

*Ricerche sulla TT38 (Gurna - Egitto) negli Archivi
di Egittologia dell'Università degli Studi di Milano*
(a.a. 2008-2009).

*La tomba di Amenemhat Surer attraverso
gli Archivi Varille dell'Università degli Studi
di Milano* (a.a. 2009-2010).

*Ricerche sul Tempio di Deir el-Medina.
Documentazione inedita negli Archivi
di Egittologia dell'Università degli Studi di Milano
(Fondo Varille)* (a.a. 2009-2010).

Alexandre Varille e le teorie simboliste
(a.a. 2010-2011).

*Bernard V. Bothmer e il principe Bibescu
negli Archivi egittologici dell'Università degli Studi
di Milano* (a.a. 2010-2011).

*Ricerche sul "causeway" del faraone Unis
a Saqqara negli Archivi Varille dell'Università
degli Studi di Milano* (a.a. 2010-2011).

Master's Degree
(Laurea magistrale e/o quadriennale)

Ricerche sui templi di File e Biga (a.a. 2005-2006).

La tomba di Pairy nella necropoli tebana (TT139)
(a.a. 2006-2007).

Ricerche sulla TT31 di Khonsu a Gurna
(a.a. 2008-2009).

Ricerche sulla TT23 di Tjay a Gurna
(a.a. 2009-2010).

*Ricerche sul Tempio di Iside a Philae negli Archivi
Egittologici dell'Università degli Studi di Milano*
(a.a. 2009-2010).

I pittori nell'Antico Egitto (a.a. 2010-2011).

*Ricerche archeologiche e filologiche sulla TT181
a Khokha (Egitto)* (a.a. 2010-2011).

DEA - Diplôme d'Études Approfondies.
École Pratique des Hautes Études,
IVᵉ Section, Paris

S. MASTROPAOLO, *Études sur les animaux
dans l'ancienne Égypte* (a.a. 2004-2005.
Under the supervision of Prof. Pascal Vernus)
[on the documents related to fauna in the Loret
Archives].

IV. *Exhibitions*

*La Biblioteca e gli Archivi di Egittologia
del Dipartimento di Scienze dell'Antichità
dell'Università degli Studi di Milano*
(Milano, Università degli Studi, 8 maggio 2002).

*Heinz Leichter (1882-1940) Südtiroler Fotograf
in Ägypten / Fotografo sudtirolese in Egitto*
(Bolzano, Galerie foto-forum,
6 novembre - 7 dicembre 2002).

Egitto. Dalle piramidi ad Alessandro Magno
(Milano, Fondazione Biblioteca di via Senato,
5 dicembre 2002 - 18 marzo 2003).

Egitto. Dalle piramidi ad Alessandro Magno
(Cremona, Museo civico Ala Ponzone e Palazzo
Stanga, 25 settembre 2004 - 28 marzo 2005).

*Il Tesoro della Statale. Collezioni e identità
di un grande Ateneo*
(Milano, Rotonda di via Besana, 23 novembre
2004 - 13 febbraio 2005).

*Victor Loret in Egypt (1881-1899).
From the Archives of the Milan University
to the Egyptian Museum in Cairo*
(Cairo, Egyptian Museum, May 19 - June 30,
2008).

The History of the Egyptian Museum
(Cairo, Egyptian Museum, October 19, 2008 -
January 31, 2009).

*Il fotografo dei faraoni: Antonio Beato in Egitto
1860-1905* (Bologna, Palazzo Comunale,
Sala d'Ercole, 9 - 29 ottobre 2008).

*Il fotografo dei faraoni: Antonio Beato in Egitto
1860-1905* (Luxor, Suzanne Mubarak Library,
14 ottobre 2009 - 15 febbraio 2010).

Kofler. Cairo 1914 (Bolzano, Espace La Stanza,
22 ottobre - 27 novembre 2010), website:
http://www.koflercairo.it/

MOSTRA FOTOGRAFICA . FOTOAUSSTELLUNG

CIRCOLO CULTURALE LA STANZA KULTURVEREIN

22.10 - 27.11.2010
VIA ORAZIO HORAZ STR. 34
BOLZANO - BOZEN

Ingresso libero - Eintritt frei

UNIVERSITÀ DEGLI STUDI DI MILANO

gefördert von
Stiftung Südtiroler Sparkasse
Fondazione Cassa di Risparmio
sostenuto da

LPS
Public Relations
Communication

Bibliography

I. *The Preservation of Antiquities*
Creation of Museums in Egypt during the Nineteenth Century
Patrizia Piacentini

D. ABOU-GHAZI, "The First Egyptian Museum", in *ASAE* 67 (1988), pp. 1-13, pls I-II.

D. ABOU-GHAZI, "The Journey of the Egyptian Museum from Boulaq to Kasr el-Nil", in *ASAE* 67 (1988), p. 16.

D. ABOU-GHAZI, "Dates in the removal from Gizah to Kasr el-Nil", in *ASAE* 67 (1988), pp. 17-18.

J. ABT, "Toward a Historian's Laboratory: The Breasted-Rockefeller Museum Projects in Egypt, Palestine, and America", in *JARCE* 33 (1996), pp. 173-194, in particular pp. 173-188.

ANONYMOUS, "Concorso Internazionale per un museo di antichità egiziane da erigersi in Cairo. Appunti e impressioni VI", in *L'Imparziale*, anno IV, 86-87 (27-28 marzo 1895), p. 2.

ANONYMOUS, "I nuovi musei, d'antichità ed arabo, al Cairo", in *L'Illustrazione italiana* XXIX, 47 (23 Novembre 1902), p. 417.

H. AUBANEL, "Au Musée de Ghizeh", in *Le Journal Égyptien* (21 Janvier 1899), p. 1.

E. B[ASILE], *Museo Egiziano. Rivista critica dei progetti esposti al concorso*, Cairo 1895.

C. BREASTED, *Pioneer to the Past: The Story of James Henry Breasted, Archaeologist*, Chicago 2009 (Reprint of the 1943 Edition with New Foreword and Photographs).

E.A.W. BUDGE, *The Nile: Notes for Travellers in Egypt*, London 1895⁴, p. 154.

J.-F. CHAMPOLLION LE JEUNE, *Lettres écrites d'Égypte et de Nubie en 1828 et 1829*, Paris 1868, pp. 382-388.

G. CHARMES, "La réorganisation du Musée de Boulaq et les études égyptologiques en France", in *Revue des deux Mondes* (1ᵉʳ Septembre 1880), pp. 209-210.

H. COLLA, *Conflicted Antiquities: Egyptology, Egyptomania, Egyptian Modernity*, Durham 2007.

M.-L. Crosnier Leconte, M. Volait (eds.), *L'Égypte d'un architecte. Ambroise Baudry (1838-1906)*, Paris 1998.

S. CURTO, "Giuseppe Botti 'primo': la vita e gli scritti", in *SEAP* 13 (1994), pp. 71-80.

É. DAVID, *Gaston Maspero. Le Gentleman égyptologue*, Paris 1999.

É. David (ed.), *G. Maspero. Lettres d'Égypte. Correspondance avec Louise Maspero [1883-1914]*, Paris 2003.

J. DE MORGAN, "Avant-propos", in [PH. VIREY], *Notice des principaux monuments exposés au Musée de Gizeh*, Le Caire 1892, pp. XVIII-XXI.

F. DE SAULCY, *Voyage en Terre-Sainte*, Paris 1865, pp. 31-42.

C. DONZEL, *En Égypte*, Paris 2007.

W. DOYON, "The Poetics of Egyptian Museum Practice", in *BMSAES* 10 (2008), pp. 1-37.

A. EDWARDS, *A Thousand Miles Up The Nile*, London 1877, p. 287.

J. F[RANZ], "Die Pläne des neuen Museums für Aegyptische Alterthümer zu Kairo", in *Deutsche Bauzeitung* (18. April 1896), pp. 197, 200-201.

É. GADY, "Les Égyptologues français au XIXᵉ siècle: quelques savants très influents", in *Revue d'histoire du XIXᵉ siècle* 32 (2006), pp. 41-62.

É. GADY, "La découverte et le projet de mise en valeur des archives du Musée Gréco-Romain d'Aléxandrie: projet AMGRA", in *EDAL* 1 (2009), pp. 141-147, pls LXV-LXVI.

É. GADY, "Un ingénieur chez les égyptologues", in F. Djindjian, C. Lorre, L. Touret (eds), *Caucase, Égypte & Perse: J. de Morgan (1857-1924), pionnier de l'aventure archéologique* (Cahiers du Musée d'Archéologie Nationale 1), Saint-Germain-en-Laye 2009, pp. 121-134.

M. GIACOMELLI, *Ernesto Basile e il concorso per il Museo di Antichità Egizie del Cairo 1894-1895*, Firenze 2010.

G.R. GLIDDON, *An Appeal to the Antiquaries of Europe on the Destruction of the Monuments of Egypt*, London 1841.

E. Godoli, M. Volait (eds), *Concours pour le musée des Antiquités égyptiennes du Caire, 1895*, Paris 2010.

Gouvernement Égyptien, *Programme du concours pour l'érection d'un musée des antiquités égyptiennes au Caire*, Le Caire 1894.

[E. GRÉBAUT, G. DARESSY], *Musée de Gizeh. Notice sommaire des monuments exposés*, Le Caire 1892.

A. HILAL, "Les premiers égyptologues égyptiens et la réforme", in A. Roussillon (ed.), *Entre réforme sociale et mouvement national: Identité et modernisation en Égypte (1882-1962)*, Le Caire 1995, pp. 340-341.

E. JAMBON, "Les fouilles de Georges Legrain dans la Cachette de Karnak (1903-1907). Nouvelles données sur la chronologie des découvertes et le destin des objets", in *BIFAO* 109 (2009), pp. 239-279, in particular notes 172-177.

H. JARITZ, "The Extension of the Egyptian Museum. A Project of 1937 by Otto Königsberger", in M. Eldamaty, M. Trad (eds), *Egyptian Museum Collections around the World*, II, Cairo 2002, pp. 581-589.

A. Jaunay (ed.), *Mémoires de Jacques de Morgan 1857-1924. Souvenirs d'un archéologue*, Paris 1997.

A. KAKOVKIN, "New Materials in Respect of Monuments Entering to Russia from Egypt in the XXᵗʰ century", in *GM* 147 (1995), pp. 61-69.

A. KHATER, *Le régime juridique des fouilles et des antiquités en Égypte*, Le Caire 1960.

M. KURZ, "Un homme d'action dans l'Égypte du XIXᵉ siècle", in LINANT DE BELLEFONDS BEY, *Voyages aux mines d'or du Pharaon*, Cognac 2002, pp. 17-101.

A. MARIETTE, *Notice des principaux monuments exposés dans les galeries provisoires du Musée d'Antiquités Égyptiennes de S. A. le Vice-Roi à Boulaq*, Alexandrie 1864.

A. MARIETTE, *Voyage dans la Haute-Egypte*, Paris-Leipzig 1893².

G. MASPERO, *Guide du visiteur du Musée de Boulaq*, Paris 1884.

G. MASPERO, "Le Musée de Boulaq a cessé d'exister", in *Journal des débats politiques et littéraires* (1ᵉʳ Mars 1890), p. 1.

G. MASPERO, "Le Musée de Boulaq et le Musée de Gizéh", in *La Nature*, XVIII année, 900 (30 Août 1890), pp. 199-202.

G. MASPERO, *Guide du visiteur au Musée du Caire*, Le Caire 1902.

G. MASPERO, "Histoire du Musée d'Antiquités du Caire", in *Revue d'Égypte et d'Orient*, 7ᵉᵐᵉ Année, 4 (1906), pp. 135-145.

G. MASPERO, *Rapports sur la marche du Service des Antiquités de 1899 à 1910*, Le Caire 1912.

G. MASPERO, in AA.VV., "Les Études Égyptologiques", in *Exposition Universelle et Internationale de San Francisco. La Science française*, II, Paris 1915, p. 24.

P. PIACENTINI, "Il contributo italiano alla tutela e alla catalogazione delle antichità nei Musei egiziani", in M. Casini (ed.), *Cento anni in Egitto. Percorsi dell'archeologia italiana*, Milano 2001, pp. 230-232, 248.

P. PIACENTINI, "Auguste Mariette in the Egyptological Archives and Library of the University of Milan", in D. Magee, J. Bourriau, S. Quirke (eds), *Sitting Beside Lepsius. Studies in Honour of Jaromir Málek at the Griffith Institute* (OLA 185), Leiden 2009, pp. 423-438.

P. PIACENTINI, V. RONDOT, "1881, musée de Boulaq, mort de Mariette", in M. Eldamaty, M. Trad (eds), *Egyptian Museum Collections around the World*, II, Cairo 2002, pp. 949-956.

E.J. POYNTER ET AL., "The Ghizeh Museum", in *The Architect and Contract Reporter* (March 16, 1894), pp. 183-184.

D.M. REID, *Whose Pharaohs? Archaeology, Museums, and Egyptian National Identity from Napoleon to World War I*, Berkeley-Los Angeles-London 2002.

A. RHONÉ, *L'Égypte à petites journées. Études et souvenirs*, Paris 1877, pp. 62-63.

H. RUGHDI, M. SAÏD, I. SIRRY, "La nouvelle loi sur les antiquités de l'Égypte et ses annexes", in *ASAE* 12 (1912), pp. 245-280.

H. SATZINGER, *Das Kunsthistorische Museum in Wien. Die Ägyptisch-Orientalische Sammlung*, Mainz am Rhein 1994, pp. 74-77.

N.S. TAMRAZ, *Nineteenth-century Cairene Houses and Palaces*, Cairo 1998.

L. VASSALLI, *I monumenti istorici egizi. Il Museo e gli scavi d'antichità eseguiti per ordine di S. A. il Viceré Ismail Pascià*, Milano 1867.

M. VOLAIT, *Fous du Caire. Excentriques, architectes & amateurs d'art en Égypte 1867-1914*, Apt 2009.

156

II. *Photographers in Egypt*
1850-1950
Laura Marucchi, Patrizia Piacentini

E. ALTMAN EVANS, *Scholars, Scoundrels, and the Sphinx: a Photographic and Archaeological Adventure up the Nile*, Nashville 2000.

S. AUBENAS, J. LACARRIÈRE, *Voyage en Orient*, Paris 2001.

M. BETRÒ (ed.), *Lungo il Nilo: Ippolito Rosellini e la Spedizione Franco-Toscana in Egitto* (Catalogue of the exhibition), Firenze 2010.

A. BLOTTIÈRE, *Egypt 1900. The View through Postcards*, Cairo 1993.

A. BLOTTIÈRE, *Vintage Egypt: Cruising the Nile in the Golden Age of Travel*, Paris 2009.

C. BREASTED, *Pioneer to the Past: The Story of James Henry Breasted, Archaeologist*, Chicago 2009 (Reprint of the 1943 Edition with New Foreword and Photographs).

J.H. BREASTED, *Egypt through the Stereoscope: A Journey through the Land of the Pharaohs*, Chicago 2010 (Reprint, New York 1900).

E. BROWN, "Les premières images par daguerreotype au monde: le photographe canadien Pierre Gustave Gaspard Joly de Lotbinière", in *L'archiviste* 118 (1999), pp. 22-29.

D. BULL, D. LORIMER, *Up the Nile: A Photographic Excursion: Egypt 1839-1898*, New York 1979.

C. BUSI, F. AMIN MOHAREB, *Fotografi in Egitto: le immagini di Heinz e Giorgio Leichter dal 1910 al 1940*, Torino 2002.

M. DEWACHTER, D. OSTER, *Un voyageur en Égypte vers 1850: "Le Nil" de Maxime Du Camp*, Paris 1987.

B. von DEWITZ, K. SCHULLER-PROCOPOVICI (eds), *Die Reise zum Nil 1849-1850. Maxime Du Camp und G. Flaubert in Ägypten, Palästina und Syrien*, Köln 1997.

C. DONZEL, *En Égypte*, Paris 2007.

W.E.N. DUNN, G.V. WORTHINGTON, *Luxor as a Health Resort*, London 1914.

A. FERRI, C. BUSI, L. MARUCCHI, P. PIACENTINI, I. ZANNIER, *Il fotografo dei faraoni: Antonio Beato in Egitto 1860-1905*, Bologna 2008.

H. GERNSHEIM, *A Concise History of Photography*, New York 1986, pp. 9-28.

M. GOLIA, *Photography and Egypt*, London 2010.

D.M. HALLER, *In Arab Lands: the Bonfils Collection of the University of Pennsylvania Museum*, Cairo 2000.

K.S. HOWE, *Félix Teynard: Calotypes of Egypt. A Catalogue Raisonné*, New York-London-Carmel 1992.

K.S. HOWE, *Excursions along the Nile: the Photographic Discovery of Ancient Egypt* (Catalogue of the exhibition), Santa Barbara 1993.

K. JACOBSON, *Odalisques & Arabesques: Orientalist Photography 1839-1925*, London 2007.

M.-T. JAMMES, A. JAMMES, *En Égypte au temps de Flaubert: 1839-1860. Les premiers photographes*, Paris 1976.

M. KHEMIR, "Le miroir et le temps. Des photographes en Égypte", in C. Menz, J.-L. Chappaz, C. Ritschard (eds), *Voyages en Égypte de l'Antiquité au début du XXᵉ siècle* (Catalogue of the exhibition), Genève 2003, pp. 259-278.

R. LUNN, *Francis Frith's Egypt and the Holy Land: the Pioneering Photographic Expeditions to the Middle East*, Salisbury, Wiltshire 2005.

S. MAYES, *The Great Belzoni. The Circus Strongman who Discovered Egypt's Ancient Treasures*, London 2003.

P. Monsel (ed.), *L'Orient des photographes Arméniens* (Catalogue of the exhibition), Paris 2007.

G.L. MUTTER, B.P. FISHMAN, "Lost Photographs of Edward L. Wilson: the American Who Documented the Discovery of the Royal Mummies Cache", in *KMT* 4 (2009-10), pp. 67-68.

D.R. NICKEL, *Francis Frith in Egypt and Palestine*, Princeton 2004.

C. ORSENIGO, "Victor Loret e Félix Guilmant nella tomba di Ramesse IX", in G. Zanetto, S. Martinelli Tempesta, M. Ornaghi (eds), *Vestigia Antiquitatis* (Quaderni di Acme 89), Milano 2007, pp. 229-237.

N.N. PEREZ, *Focus East: Early Photography in the Near East, 1839-1885*, New York 1988.

P. PIACENTINI, *L'antico Egitto di Napoleone*, Milano 2000.

P. PIACENTINI, "La biblioteca di Alexandre Varille e le prime fotografie aeree dell'Egitto", in C. Basile, A. Di Natale (eds), *Atti del VII Convegno Nazionale di Egittologia e Papirologia, Siracusa, 29 novembre-2 dicembre 2001* (Quaderni del Museo del Papiro 11), Siracusa 2003, pp. 133-143.

S. PLANTUREUX, *Vingt-quatre épreuves originales de Théodule Devéria*, Paris [2002].

G. RÉVEILLAC, "Les collections photographiques Beato, Gaddis-Seif, Adly-Leichter", in *Cahiers de Karnak* 11 (2003), pp. 515-524, pls I-IX.

G. RÉVEILLAC, "Le fonds Gaddis. Deux photographes égyptiens à Louqsor (1910-1930)", in C. Menz, J.-L. Chappaz, C. Ritschard (eds), *Voyages en Égypte* ... cit., pp. 279-286.

C. RITSCHARD, "L'artiste et son modèle: Le voyage des images", in C. Menz, J.-L. Chappaz, C. Ritschard (eds), *Voyages en Égypte* ... cit., pp. 295-307.

J.-C. SIMOËN, *Égypte éternelle: les voyageurs photographes au siècle dernier*, Paris 1993.

A. von SPECHT (ed.), *Lepsius, Die deutsche Expedition en den Nil* (Catalogue of the exhibition), Kairo 2006.

J. THOMPSON, *Edward William Lane 1801-1876: The Life of the Pioneering Egyptologist and Orientalist*, Cairo 2010.

L. THORNTON, *Les Orientalistes. Peintres voyageurs*, Courbevoie (Paris) 1994.

N. TUCCELLI, G. RÉVEILLAC, *Le Nil en dahabieh 1850-1914*, Paris 2001.

R. VERGNIEUX, "La carte postale en Égypte au début du XXᵉ siècle", in C. Menz, J.-L. Chappaz, C. Ritschard (eds), *Voyages en Égypte* ... cit., pp. 287-294.

W.M. WEISS, N. MACHFUS, *Im Land der Pharaonen: Ägypten in historischen Fotos von Lehnert und Landrock*, Heidelberg 2004.

I. ZANNIER, *L'Egitto del Grand Tour nella fotografia degli Zangaki*, Milano 1999.

III. *Aspects of Ancient Egypt in Nineteenth Century Painting*
Fernando Mazzocca

H. DE MEULENAERE, *L'Égypte Ancienne dans la Peinture du XIXᵉ siècle*, Bruxelles 1992.

J.-M. HUMBERT, *L'Égyptomanie dans l'Art Occidental*, Paris 1989, pp. 228-275.

J.-M. Humbert, M. Pantazzi, C. Ziegler (eds), *Egyptomania. L'Égypte dans l'art occidental 1730 -1930* (Catalogue of the exhibition), Paris 1994.

C. Menz, C. Ritschard (eds), *Cléopâtre. Dans le miroir de l'art occidental* (Catalogue of the exhibition), Genève 2004.

IV. *Walls and Dishes*
Gaetano Lodi, an Italian Painter for the Khedive Ismail Pasha
Patrizia Piacentini

AA.VV., *Il Teatro di Gaetano Lodi, 1881-1981. Centenario del Teatro Comunale di Crevalcore*, Crevalcore 1981.

Accademia Indifferenti Risoluti (ed.), *Gaetano Lodi*, Bologna 1987.

ANONYMOUS, "Our Roman Letter", in *New Zeland Tablet*, Rorahi VII, Putanga 355 (February 6, 1880), p. 17.

ANONYMOUS, "English News", in *New Zeland Tablet*, Rorahi VI, Putanga 345 (May 5, 1880), p. 7.

G. BANDINI, "Esempi di ceramica 'egittizzante' nell'Ottocento italiano", in F. Longo, C. Zaccagnini (eds), *Il fascino dell'Egitto nell'Italia dell'Ottocento. La collezione di Cortona e la diffusione del gusto egittizzante*, Atti della giornata di studio: Cortona 3 maggio 2003, Cortona 2005, pp. 97-114.

E. BETTIO, O. RUCELLAI, *Archivio Storico Richard-Ginori della Manifattura di Doccia* (Quaderni di Archimeetings 16), Firenze 2007.

S. CHINI, "Il servito per il Khédive d'Egitto della Manifattura Ginori di Doccia", in L. Casprini Gentile, D. Liscia Bemporad (eds), *Il gusto esotico nella Manifattura di Doccia*, Firenze 2008 (where the design of the service is not attributed to Lodi by mistake).

F. DE FILIPPIS, *Storie Napoletane d'Altri Tempi*, Napoli 1959, pp. 125-126.

N. FERRIANI, "Gaetano Lodi: dalle decorazioni in Egitto alla Cooperativa di Imola", in *Rassegna storica crevalcorese* 1 (2005), pp. 35-54.

R. LA GUARDIA, "Luigi Vassalli e il suo archivio privato nelle Civiche Raccolte Archeologiche di Milano", in EAD. ET AL., *L'egittologo Luigi Vassalli (1812-1887). Disegni e documenti nei Civici Istituti Culturali Milanesi*, Milano 1994, pp. 13-15, 39-40.

L. FIGUIER, *Le meraviglie dell'industria. I. Il vetro e le porcellane. Il cristallo, le majoliche, le porcellane. Traduzione autorizzata dall'autore, con numerose aggiunte per la parte italiana*, Milano 1880², p. 302, figs 234-237.

L. Gendre (ed.), *Réminiscences d'Égypte ...*, Sèvres, Paris 1994.

L. GINORI LISCI, *Le porcellane di Doccia*, Firenze-Milano 1963, pl. LXXX.

G. LIVERANI, *Il Museo delle porcellane di Doccia*, Milano 1967, pp. 44, 74, pl. CXIV.

A. MINGHETTI, *Enciclopedia Biografica e Bibliografica Italiana*, Milano 1939, p. 258, *s.v.* "Ceramisti".

R. Monti (ed.), *La manifattura Richard-Ginori di Doccia*, Milano 1988, pp. 91-93.

E. PIERI, "Architetti e artigiani tra Toscana ed Egitto nella seconda metà dell'Ottocento", in M.A. Giusti, E. Godoli (eds), *L'orientalismo nell'architettura italiana tra Ottocento e Novecento*, Atti del convegno internazionale di studi, Viareggio 23-25 ottobre 1997, Siena 1999, pp. 301-310.

C. RAVANELLI GUIDOTTI, "Gaetano Lodi (1830-1886) un ornatista per l'arte della ceramica", in *Faenza* 1-6, LXVII (1981), pp. 83-91.

C. RAVANELLI GUIDOTTI, *Società Cooperativa Ceramica di Imola. Centovent'anni di opere*, I, Milano 1994.

G. RICCI, "Gaetano Lodi", in *Il Comune di Bologna* 3 (1932), pp. 19-29.

O. RUCELLAI, "La manifattura Ginori nell'Ottocento. Lo sviluppo industriale e le 'ceramiche artistiche'", in A. Biancalana (ed.), *Quando la manifattura diventa arte. Le porcellane e le maioliche di Doccia*, Atti del convegno, Lucca 7 maggio 2003 (Accademia lucchese di scienze, lettere e arti, saggi e ricerche 8), Pisa 2005, pp. 31-52.

C. UGOLINI, "La 'saletta egizia' di Gaetano Lodi in Palazzo Sanguinetti", in *L'Archiginnasio* 99 (2004), pp. 309-342.

Wannenes Art Auctions, *Argenti, gioielli, una collezione di maioliche e porcellane di Doccia, Genova, 17 maggio 2010*, cat. n. 84.

V. *Egypt as an Allegory of the Modern Age*
Political Satire, Illustration, and Imagérie populaire
Antonello Negri, Marta Sironi

E. Balzaretti, E. Cavalleris, E. D'Amicone (eds), *Fumetti d'Egitto. L'Egitto dei faraoni nel mondo del fumetto*, Milano 1994.

G.A. CESANA, *Da Firenze a Suez e viceversa. Impressioni di viaggio di G.A. Cesana*, Firenze 1870.

A. FERRERO, E. DE AMICIS, *1856-1897. Caricature di Teja (dal Pasquino)*, Torino 1900.

T. Groensteen (ed.), *L'Égypte dans la bande dessinée* (Catalogue of the exhibition), Angoulême 1998.

P. Pallottino (ed.), *L'occhio della tigre. Alberto Della Valle fotografo e illustratore salgariano*, Palermo 1994.

VI. *Egypt in the Box*
Pharaonic Inspiration in Everyday Life
Patrizia Piacentini

AA.VV., *L'Egitto in Europa* (*L'Erasmo. Bimestrale della civiltà europea* 13), Milano 2003, pp. 4-103.

B. BRIER, *Egyptomania. Hillwood Art Museum* (Catalogue of the exhibition), Brookville 1992.

P. Connor (ed.), *The Inspiration of Egypt: Its Influence on British Artists, Travellers and Designers, 1700-1900* (Catalogue of the exhibition), Brighton 1983.

J.S. CURL, *Egyptomania. The Egyptian Revival: a Recurring Theme in the History of Taste*, Manchester-New York 1994 (augmented ed.).

J.S. CURL, *The Egyptian Revival: Ancient Egypt as the Inspiration for Design Motifs in the West*, Abingdon-New York 2005.

B. CURRAN, *The Egyptian Renaissance: The Afterlife of Ancient Egypt in Early Modern Italy*, Chicago-London 2007.

N. DALE REEVE, S. FOOTE, A. ROBIN, *Egyptian Revival Jewelry and Design*, Atglen, Penn. 2007.

S. De Caro (ed.), *Egittomania: Iside e il mistero* (Catalogue of exhibition), Milano 2006.

D. FLETCHER, *The Baldwin Styles: The Colour & Architecture of US Locomotives*, I, *The Origins of the American Locomotive Architecture*, available at http://www.pacificng.com/template.php?page=/ref/blw/style/baldwinstyles.htm

W. GOTH REGIER, *Book of the Sphinx*, Phoenix Mill 2005.

B. HANDY, "Watch like an Egyptian", in *Vanity Fair* (January 29, 2008), available at http://www.vanityfair.com/culture/features/2008/01/egyptomania200801?currentPage=1

M. HARITATOS, P. GIAKOUMAKIS, *A History of the Greek Cigarette*, Athens 1997.

H. HERZER, S. SCHOSKE, R. WEDEWER, D. WILDUNG, *Ägyptische und Moderne Skulptur: Aufbruch und Dauer* (Catalogue of the exhibition), München 1986.

J.-M. HUMBERT, *L'Égyptomanie dans l'Art Occidental*, Paris 1989.

J.-M. Humbert (ed.), *L'égyptomanie à l'épreuve de l'archéologie: actes du colloque international organisé au musée du Louvre les 8 et 9 avril 1994*, Paris-Bruxelles 1996.

J.-M. Humbert, M. Pantazzi, C. Ziegler (eds), *Egyptomania. L'Égypte dans l'art occidental 1730-1930* (Catalogue of the exhibition), Paris 1994.

S. MacDonald, M. Rice (eds), *Consuming ancient Egypt* (*Encounters with ancient Egypt*), London-Portland OR 2003.

C. MULLEN, *Cigarette Pack Art*, London 1979.

H. NAVRÁTILOVÁ, *Egyptian Revival in Bohemia 1850-1920. Orientalism and Egyptomania in Czech Lands*, Praha 2003.

P. PIACENTINI, "Nefertiti postmoderna", in *Archeo* 60 (1990), pp. 118-120.

P. PIACENTINI, "Follie d'Egitto", in *Archeo* 111 (1994), pp. 90-95.

H. PLAZA-MANNING, "Mummies & Sphinxes & Scarabs, Oh My! Egyptianizing Desing in America" in *KMT* 19/1 (Spring 2008), pp. 77-82.

T. PORTERFIELD, *The Allure of the Empire: Art in the Service of French Imperialism 1798-1836*, Princeton NJ 1998.

J. Putnam, W.V. Davies (eds), *Time Machine: Ancient Egypt and Contemporary Art at the British Museum*, London 1994.

D.P. RYAN, "Cleopatra Had a Jazz Band. Egypt in Early 20ᵗʰ Century Sheet Music" in *KMT* 18/1 (Spring 2007), pp. 73-80.

J. RUDOE, "Cartier and the passion for Egypt", in *British Museum Magazine* 29 (1997), pp. 2-5.

R. SHECHTER, "Selling Luxury: The Rise of the Egyptian Cigarette and the Transformation of the Egyptian Tobacco Market, 1850-1914", in *International Journal of Middle East Studies* 35/1 (2003), pp. 51-75.

P. VERNUS, *Dictionnaire amoureux de l'Égypte pharaonique*, Paris 2009, pp. 299-334, *s.v.* "Égyptomanie", "Égyptophilie".

D. WILDUNG, M. WULLEN, I. WENDERHOLM, *Hieroglyphen! Der Mythos der Bilderschrift von Nofretete bis Andy Wharol* (Catalogue of the exhibition), Berlin-Köln 2005.

Index of Names and Places

Sara Mastropaolo, Christian Orsenigo

Dates indicated are only for persons no longer alive when we were able to determine them.
For the Egyptian kings, also see the Chronology.
"Egyptological Archives and Library (Milan)" and "Università degli Studi di Milano" are not indexed, since mentioned in almost all the pages of the book.

Abbas Pasha Hilmi II (1874-1944): 6, 21, 26
Abd el-Hamid, Ahmed (active in the 1970s): 29
Abdin Palace (Cairo): 24, 26
Abouroasch *see* Abu Rawash
Abu Rawash: 17
    Abydos: 46
    Temple of Sety I: 46
Académie des Inscriptions et Belles-Lettres (Paris): 46
Académie des Sciences (Paris): 45
Accademia delle Belle Arti di Brera (Milan): 75, 76
Accademia di Belle Arti (Bologna): 87, 92, 113
Accademia di Francia (Rome): 78
Accademia Fiorentina (Florence): 92
Africa: 50, 82, 92
African Cigarette Company: 136
Ahmed Effendi *see* Kamal Ahmed
Aida: 104
Akhenaton: 134
Alessandria *see* Alexandria
Alexandria: IX, 17, 28, 50, 54, 61, 132, 136
    Graeco-Roman Museum: IX, 17, 20
    Pompey's Column: 50
Alexandrie *see* Alexandria
Alfieri Collection (APICE): 122
Algeria: 61, 64
Alma-Tadema (Sir), Lawrence (1836-1912): 75, 80, 82, 134
Ambar Cigarettes: 132, 134
Amenhotep II (18th Dynasty): 23
Amenhotep Huy: 134
Aménophis II *see* Amenhotep II
America *see* United States of America
Amsterdam: 80, 136
    Rijksmuseum: 80
Angelelli, Giuseppe (1803-1844): 76
Anglo-Egyptian Cigarette & Tobacco Co.: 136
Angoletta, Bruno (1889-1954): 124
Antiquities Service *see* Egyptian Antiquities Service
Antwerp: 82
    Musée Royal des Beaux-Arts: 82
APICE (Archivi della Parola, dell'Immagine e della Comunicazione Editoriale, Milano): IX, X, 120, 122, 124
    Alfieri Collection: 122
    Grandini Collection: 124
    Marengo Collection: 120, 122
    Sergio Reggi '900 Collection: 122, 124
Arab League (Palace of, Cairo): 23
Arago, François (1786-1853): 45
Archer, Frederick Scott (1813-1857): 46
Arnoux, Hippolyte (active 1860s-1900): 54, 61, 68
Ars Libri (Boston): 68
Asia: 92
Associazione Per-megiat onlus per la tutela e la valorizzazione delle Biblioteche sull'antico Egitto: 131, 132, 134, 136
    Rus E. Gant Collection: 132, 134, 136
Assouan *see* Aswan
Aswan: 17
    Aswan dam: 82
Asyut: 17
Athens: 54
Aubanel, Henry (active last decades 19th century): 21
Austria: 12
Austro-Hungarian Empire: 24
Autriche *see* Austria
Avenue of the Sphinxes (Karnak): 54

Bab el-Nasr (Cairo): 5
Badiali, Giuseppe (ca.1798-ca.1859): 87
Baedeker, Karl (1801-1859): 24, 29
Baldwin (locomotives): 131
Banca d'Italia (Bologna): 87
Banca d'Italia (Florence, Stanza Ottagonale): 92
Bargoût (Mariette's dog): 13
Barguet, Paul (1915- ?): 68
Barsanti, Alessandro (1858-1917): 26
Basile, Ernesto (1857-1932): 24
Baudelaire, Charles Pierre (1821-1867): 120
Baudry, Ambroise (1838-1906): 20, 26, 92, 94, 104
Baudry, Paul (1828-1886): 87, 92
Beato, Antonio (1832-1906): 61, 62, 64, 68
Béchard, Émile (active 1870s-1880s): 46
Béchard, Hénri (active 1870s-1880s): 46
Becheroni, Lorenzo Junior (active second half 19th century): 94
Bedford, Francis (1816-1894): 50
Beirut: 54
Belluno: 76
Belzoni, Giovanni Battista (1778-1823): 45, 78
Bendassi, Giuseppe (active second half 19th century): 94
Benecke, Ernest (1817-1894): 46
Berlin: 136
Biban el Molouk *see* Valley of the Kings
Biblioteca dell'Archiginnasio (Bologna): 113
Birmingham: 78
    Birmingham City Museum and Art Galleries: 78
Bissing, Friedrich Wilhelm von (1873-1956): 26, 29
Blechman, Robert Oscar: 124
Bodourian Egyptian Cigarettes: 136
Bologna: X, 61, 87, 92, 94, 104, 106, 113
    Accademia di Belle Arti: 87, 92, 113
    Banca d'Italia: 87
    Biblioteca dell'Archiginnasio: 113
    Caffè del Corso (Sala delle Signore): 87
    Istituzione Galleria d'Arte Moderna: 87
    Museo Internazionale e Biblioteca della Musica: 113
    Palazzo Bonora: 87
    Palazzo Dal Monte: 87
    Palazzo Rossi: 87
    Palazzo Sanguinetti (Saletta Egizia): 106, 113
    Real Accademia Centrale: 92
    Theater Eleonora Duse (former Teatro Brunetti): 87
Bolzano: 62
Bonaparte, Josephine (1763-1814): 94
Bonfils, Paul-Félix (1831-1885): 6, 50, 54, 64
Bonnefoy, Henry-Arthur (1839-1917): 10
Borchardt, Ludwig (1863-1938): 29
Bosnia: 24
Boston: 68, 78
    Museum of Fine Arts: 78
Botanic Museum (Cairo): 20
Bothmer, Bernard V. (1912-1993): 28, 70
    Bothmer Collection: 29, 64
Botti, Antonio (1875-1963): 17
Botti, Augusto (1891-1919): 20
Botti, Carlo (1840-1923): 17
Botti, Giuseppe "the First" (1853-1903): IX, 14, 17, 20
    Botti Collection: 17
Boulak *see* Bulaq
Boulaq *see* Bulaq
Bowring (Lord), John (1792-1872): 6
Breasted, James Henry (1865-1935): 28, 29, 68
Brera Crüwell-Tabak (cigarettes): 134, 136
Breslau: 136
Bristol: 136
British Museum (London): 80, 82
Brogi, Giacomo (1822-1881): 87
Brugsch, Émile (1842-1930): 13, 17, 26, 29, 46
Brugsch, Heinrich (1827-1894): 6, 13
Brussels *see* Bruxelles
Bruxelles: 136
Buccellati, Graziella: X
Budge (Sir), Ernest Alfred Thompson Wallis (1857-1934): 21
Bulaq (Cairo): IX, 6, 10, 14, 20, 21

Bulaq harbour: 10
Bulaq Museum: IX, 6, 10, 12, 13, 14, 17, 20, 21, 46, 104, 134
    Engineers School: 6
Busi (active in the 1870s): 104

Cabanel, Alexandre (1823-1889): 82, 134
Cadart, Alfred (1828-1875): 75
Caffè del Corso (Bologna, Sala delle Signore): 87
Cairo: IX, X, 5, 6, 12, 13, 20, 24, 26, 28, 29, 46, 50, 54, 61, 62, 64, 92, 94, 104, 132, 134, 136
    Abdin Palace: 24, 26
    Bab el-Nasr: 5
    Botanic Museum: 20
    Bulaq: 6, 10, 13, 14, 17, 20, 21
    Bulaq harbour: 10
    Bulaq Museum: IX, 6, 10, 12, 13, 14, 17, 20, 21, 46, 104, 134
    Cairo University (faculty of engineering): 23
    Citadel: 6
    Coptic Museum: 20
    (Egyptian) Museum: IX, 14, 24, 26, 28, 29, 62
    Entomologic Museum: 20
    Ethnographic Museum: 20
    Ezbekieh: 5, 6, 13
    Ezbekieh square: 23
    Fustat: 29
    Geologic Museum: 20
    Gezireh island: 10, 23
    Islamic Museum: 20
    Ismailiya square (now Tahrir): 23
    Kasr-en-Nil: 28
    Mohamed Ali's Mosque: 6
    Mousky: 13
    National Museum of Egyptian Civilization (Fustat): 29
    Nile Hilton Hotel: 23
    Opera House: 104
    Palace of the Arab League: 23
    Parliament: 26
    Sale Room (Egyptian Museum): 26, 28, 29
    Sayedah Zeinab area: 6
    Shepheard's Hotel: 6, 26, 50, 61, 132, 134
    Tahrir Square: IX, 20, 23, 24, 29
    zoo: 20
Cambray Digny, Guglielmo (1820-1906): 122
Camel (cigarettes): 122
Capart, Jean (1877-1947): 68
CARIPLO Foundation: X
Cartier (jewellery): 131
Castelfranco Emilia: 87
Cavalla *see* Kavalla
Caviglia, Giovanni Battista (1770-1845): 5
Cento: 87
Cesana, Giuseppe Augusto (1821-1903): 120, 122
Cesari (assistant of Jafet Torelli, 19th century): 94
Champollion, Jean-François (1790-1832): 5, 45, 76, 78
Chapchal Frères Manifacturers: 134, 136
Chassinat, Émile Gaston (1868-1948): 29
Chephren (4th Dynasty): 6, 10
    Valley Temple (Giza): 6, 10
Chicago: 62
    The Oriental Institute: 62
Christofle, Charles (1805-1863): 92
Cicolani, Pietro (active second half 19th century): 94
Citadel (Cairo): 6
Cleopatra VII Philopator (51-30 BC): 82, 134, 136
Cleopatra soap: 132
Collège de France (Paris): 68
Colossi of Memnon: 50
Compagnie du Canal de Suez: 54
Compagnie du transit *see* Nile Navigation Company (Bulaq)
Constantinople: 54
Cooperativa Ceramica d'Imola (Imola): 113
Cooper-Hewitt Museum (New York): 94, 104
Coptic Museum (Cairo): 20
Correnti, Cesare (1815-1888): 104
Crevalcore: 87, 94, 104, 106, 113
Crüwell Spezialfabrik: 136
Crystal Palace (London): 80

Daguerre, Louis Jacques Mandé (1787-1851): 45
Dahshur: 70
Dandolo, Tullio (1801-1870): 76
Daressy, George Émile (1864-1938): 26, 68
Decleva, Enrico: X
Deir el-Bahri (first cache): 14, 17
Deir el-Medina: X
    Tomb of Pashed (TT 3): X
Délié, Hippolyte (active 1860s-1880s): 46
Della Valle, Alberto (1851-1928): 124
de Martino, Giuseppe (italian consul, active
    second half 19th century): 94
DeMille, Cecil B. (1881-1959): 78
de Morgan, Jacques Jean Marie (1857-1924): 21,
    23, 24, 26, 29
Denon (Baron), Dominique Vivant (1747-1825): 78
Depretis, Agostino (1813-1887): 122
Deutsch, Ludwig (1855-1935): 50
Devéria, Théodule (1831-1871): 13, 46
Diez, Julius (1870-1957): 122
Diodorus (1st century BC): 78
Disney, Walter Elias (1901-1966): 124
Dittrich, P. (active 1880-1918): 50, 54
Dix, Otto (1891-1969): 124
Doccia: X, 94, 104, 113
Doré, Gustave (1832-1883): 78
Dourgnon, Marcel (1858-1911): 24, 26
Du Camp, Maxime (1822-1894): 46
Duchesne, Alexandre Adolphe (1797-post 1829):
    76
Dumas, Tancrède (1830-1905): 54
Dunn, William Edward Nickolls (1871-1925): 68
Dutertre, André (1753-1842): 75

Ebers, Georg Moritz (1837-1898): 62, 80
Edel, Elmar (1914-1997)
    Edel Collection: 17, 45, 54, 64
Edinburgh: 78
Ed. Laurens (cigarettes): 136
Edward VII (1841-1910): 50, 106
Edwards, Amelia (1831-1892): 13
Egitto see Egypt
Egypt: IX, X, 1, 3, 5, 6, 10, 13, 14, 17, 20, 21,
    23, 24, 26, 43, 45, 46, 50, 54, 61, 62, 64,
    68, 71, 73, 75, 76, 78, 80, 82, 92, 94, 106,
    117, 119, 120, 122, 124, 127, 129, 131,
    132, 134, 136
Égypte see Egypt
Egyptian Antiquities Service: 5, 6, 14, 17, 20, 21,
    23, 26, 28, 29, 62, 68, 92
Egyptian Cigarette and Tobacco Manufactory: 136
Egyptian Cigarette Company: 136
Egyptian Court (Crystal Palace, London): 80
Egyptian Museum (Cairo): IX, 14, 24, 26, 28, 29,
    62
Egyptian Museum (Turin): 120
El Adly, Hassan Ahmed (1908-1980): 64
Elfy Bey (?-1807): 6
el-Tahtawi, Rifaa (1801-1871): 6
England: 24, 50, 106, 122, 132
Entomologic Museum (Cairo): 20
Esna: 54, 132
    Temple: 54, 132
Ethnographic Museum (Cairo): 20
Europa see Europe
Europe: 10, 12, 13, 23, 50, 76, 92, 120
Ezbekieh (Cairo): 5, 6, 13
Ezbekieh square (Cairo): 23
Ezbekyeh see Ezbekieh

Faccioli, Raffaele (1845-1916): 94
Fakhry, Husayn (1843-1910): 23
Faruffini, Federico (1831-1869): 75, 76
Favrod, Collezione (Raccolte Musei Fratelli
    Alinari): 87
Fayoum: 17
Félix, Lecomte (1795-1870) – pseudonym for
    Louis-François Raban de Damville: 122
Ferrara: 87
Figuier, Luigi G. (1819-1894): 94, 104, 106
Finette (Mariette's gazelle): 13

Fioravanti Cigarettes: 132, 134
Fiorelli, Giuseppe (1823-1896): 104
Fiorillo, Luigi (active 1870s-1890): 61, 68
Flaubert, Gustave (1821-1880): 46
Florence: 76, 87, 92, 94, 104, 106
    Accademia Fiorentina: 92
    Banca d'Italia (Stanza Ottagonale): 92
    Museo Archeologico: 76, 104
    Raccolte Musei Fratelli Alinari: 87
Floris, Michel Ange (active 19th century): 10, 104
France: 5, 24, 76, 92, 122, 132
Fraser, George Willoughby (1866-1923): 23
    Fraser Collection: 23
Freyha (cigarettes): 134, 136
Frith, Francis (1822-1898): 50
Fuad I, King (1868-1936): 28, 64, 68
Furniss, Harry (1854-1925): 120
Fustat (Cairo): 29
    National Museum of Egyptian Civilization: 29

Gaddis, Attaya (1893-1972): 64
Gaddis Photo Store: 64
Galioubieh: 5
Galleria Nazionale d'Arte Moderna (Rome): 75
Galleria Vittorio Emanuele II (Milan): X, 87, 92
Gant, Rus E. Collection: 132, 134, 136
Garozzo, Giuseppe (1847-?): 20, 26
Gautier, Théophile (1811-1872): 80, 82
GEM (Grand Egyptian Museum, Giza): 29
Geologic Museum (Cairo): 20
Georgiladakis (active last decades 19th century): 54
Germany: 24, 122, 132
Gerôme, Jean-Léon (1824-1904): 82
Gezireh island (Cairo): 10, 23
Ginori (factory): X, 94
Ginori Lisci, Carlo Benedetto (1851-1905): 106
Ginori Lisci, Lorenzo (1823-1878): 106
Giovannetti, Eugenio (1883-1951): 122
Giza: IX, X, 6, 10, 13, 17, 20, 21, 26, 28, 29, 50,
    61, 70, 134
    Chephren's Valley Temple: 6, 10
    GEM (Grand Egyptian Museum): 29
    Giza Museum: IX, X, 20, 21, 23, 28, 29
        Sale Room: 28, 29
    Giza Palace: X, 20, 21, 23, 26, 28, 87, 92, 94
    Great Pyramid: 14, 61
    Pyramids: 13, 17, 20, 29, 134,
    Sphinx: 10, 14, 132
    Temple d'Armachis: 6, 10
Gizeh see Giza
Gliddon, George Robins (1809-1857): 6
Goupil-Fesquet, Frédéric (1817-1878): 45
Graeco-Roman Museum (Alexandria): IX, 17, 20
Grande Piramide see Great Pyramid
Grandini Collection (APICE): 124
Grandville - pseudonym of Jean-Ignace-Isidore
    Gérard (1803-1847): 119, 120
Great Pyramid (Giza): 61
Grébaut Eugène (1846-1915): 20
Greece: 24, 80, 82, 132
Green, John Beasly (1832-1856): 46
Guignet, Adrien (1816-1854): 80
Guilmant, Félix Alexandre (1837-1911): 62
Guiragossian, Abraham (active first decades
    20th century): 54

Hadges Nessim (cigarettes): 136
Halpaus Aclesto (cigarettes): 134, 136
Hapsburgs (family): 82
Hathor: 134
Haydon, Benjamin (1786-1846): 78
Heidar, Hussein Bey (active first half 19th century):
    5
Hekekian, Yusuf Bey (1807-1875): 6
Heliopolis: 50
    Obelisk of Senuseret I: 50
Hermes Mixed Egyptian Cigarettes: 134, 136
Herodotus (ca 484 BC-ca 425 BC): 78
Hetepheres: 29
Heymann, Laroche & Co. (second half 19th
    century): 54

Holland: 24
Hollywood: 78, 122
Holy Land: 10
Horeau, Hector (1801-1872): 45
Hosni, Hassan (active 19th century): 17
Hubert (Austrian consul, active first half 19th
    century): 12

Imola: 92
    Cooperativa Ceramica d'Imola: 113
    Palazzo Vacchi: 92
India: 106, 132
Institut de France (Paris): 29
International Exhibition (London): 50
Isis: 124, 134
Islamic Museum (Cairo): 20
Ismail Pasha (1830-1895): X, 12, 13, 20, 23, 85, 87,
    92, 94, 104, 106, 113, 122, 132
Ismailiya square (now Tahrir, Cairo): 23
Issa, Mohamed (active end 19th-beginning 20th
    century): 26
Isthmus of Suez see Suez Canal
Istituzione Galleria d'Arte Moderna (Bologna): 87
Istmo di Suez see Suez Canal
Italia (ship): 122
Italia see Italy
Italy: X, 17, 24, 75, 87, 92, 94, 104, 120, 122

Jerusalem: 61
John Soane Museum (London): 78
Joly de Lotbinière, Gaspard-Pierre-Gustave
    (1798-1865): 45
Jugend: 122
Junghaendel, Max (1861-?): 62

Kais. Kön. Tabak Regie (cigarettes): 134, 136
Kamal, Ahmed (Effendi, Pacha, 1851-1923): 17, 21
Karnak: 12, 54, 64, 68, 134
    Avenue of the Sphinxes: 54
    Great Temple: 64, 134
Kasr-en-Nil (Cairo): 28
Kavalla: 132, 136
Khartoum: 136
Kitchener (Lord), Horatio Herbert (1850-1916): 50
Kodak laboratory (Cairo): 64
Kofler (active first decades of the 20th century): IX,
    68
Koln: 136
Kom Ombo: 17, 46
    Temple: 46
Königsberger Otto (1908-1999): 29
Kunsthistorisches Museum (Vienna): 6

Lacau, Pierre (1873-1963): 26, 29, 64, 68
    Lacau Collection: IX, 17, 28, 29, 68
Laka Joko - pseudonym of Harry Furniss: 120
Lane, Edward William (1801-1876): 45
Laroche, Antoine (active 19th century): 54
Léandre, Charles Lucien (1862-1939): 122
Lebanon: 64
Le Caire see Cairo
Leclant, Jean: 64
Lecomte du Noüy, Jules-Jean-Antoine (1842-1923):
    82
Legrain, Georges (1865-1917): 5, 62
Leichter, Georges (active until 1940): 62
Leichter, Heinz (1882-1940): 62, 64, 68
    Leichter Collection: 68
Leichter's Photo Store: 62
Lekegian, Gabriel (active 1887-1925): 6, 50
Leoni, Camillo (1830-1907): 87
Lepsius, Karl Richard (1810-1884): 45, 76
Lerebours, Noël Paymal (1807-1873): 45
Le Rire: 122
Lesseps, Ferdinand de (1805-1894): 6
Liban: 136
Liebig (trade cards): 132
L'Imparziale: 24
Linant de Bellefonds, Maurice-Adolphe
    (1800-1883): 6

Lissa: 122
Livorno: 87, 94
Lodi, Cesare Francesco (second half 19th century): 92, 104
Lodi, Gaetano (1830-1886): X, 23, 85, 87, 92, 94, 104, 106, 113, 131
Lodi, Linda Maddalena Maria (second half 19th century): 104
Lodi, Luigi Scipione (second half 19th century): 92, 104
Lodi, Messeri Maria (19th century): 92, 104
Lombardy: IX
London: 45, 46, 50, 78, 82, 106, 120, 131, 136
    British Museum: 80, 82
    Crystal Palace (Egyptian Court): 80
    International Exhibition: 50
    John Soane Museum: 78
    Piccadilly: 45
    Royal Collection: 106
    Universal Exhibition: 82
Loret, Victor (1859-1946): 14, 17, 23, 26, 62, 64, 131
    Loret Collection: IX, X, 14, 17, 23, 131
Lotbinière, Gaspard-Pierre-Gustave Joly de (1798-1865): 45
Louis XVI (1754-1793): 92
Louvre see Musée du Louvre
Luxor: 28, 54, 61, 62, 64, 68, 136
    Luxor Hotel: 62
    Suzanne Mubarak Library: 61
    Temple: 62, 68
    Winter Palace: 64
Lybia: 64

Maat: 46
Malta: 24, 68
    Saint Clement (internment camp): 68
Makart, Hans (1840-1884): 82
Manetti, Benedetta: X
Manfredini, Giuseppe: 87
Mansourah: 17
Marciano, Nicola (1837-?): 26
Marengo Collection (APICE): 120, 122
Mariette, Auguste-Édouard (1821-1881): 6, 10, 12, 13, 14, 17, 20, 21, 23, 26, 46, 92, 132, 134
Marquis & Fiorillo (active last decades 19th century): 61
Martin, John (1789-1854): 78
Marucchi, Laura: IX, 43, 45
Maspero (Sir), Gaston Camille Charles (1846-1916): 10, 14, 17, 20, 26, 28, 62
Maspero, Louise (1859-1952): 17
Maximilian, Ferdinand Joseph, Archduke of Austria (1832-1867): 6
Maximilian Joseph, Duke of Bavaria (1808-1888): 45
Mazzocca, Fernando: IX, 73, 75
Mecca: 61, 127
Mehmet Ali see Mohamed Ali Pacha
Meissner (active 1860s): 50
Melachrino, Miltiades (1847-1934): 134
Melchisedecca: 127
Memphis: 13, 94, 119
Memphis Design Group: 94
Menabrea, Luigi Federico (1809-1896): 122
Mengoni, Fontanelice Giuseppe (1829-1877): 92
Méry, Joseph (1797-1866): 122
Métivet, Lucien (1863-1930): 122
Metropolitan Museum of Art (New York): 131
Metz, Jean de – pseudonym of Mme Benjamin Arthaud née Marie Thérèse Rey: 5
Milan: X, 75, 87, 92, 104
    Accademia delle Belle Arti di Brera: 75, 76
    Galleria Vittorio Emanuele II: X, 87, 92
    Pinacoteca di Brera: 76
Milla (cigarettes): 136
Milos (island): 61
Mimaut, Jean-François (1774-1837): 5
Minghetti, Angelo (1822-1885): 87
Minia: 17
Mission Archéologique Française: 14
Mitry, Philip E.: 132, 134

M. Melachrino & Co. (cigarettes): 134, 136
Modena: 17, 87, 106
Mohamed Ali's Mosque (Cairo): 6
Mohamed Ali Pasha (1769-1849): 5, 6, 13, 132
Mohamed Said Pacha (1822-1863): 6, 10, 12, 13
Mohamed Tawfiq (1852-1892): 21
Montabone, Luigi (died 1877): 94, 104
Montreal: 136
Morès (active first decades 20th century): 64, 68
Morocco: 64
Moses: 122
Mousky (Cairo): 13
Mubarak Library (Luxor): see Suzanne Mubarak Library
Munich: 45
Musée de Boulaq see Bulaq Museum (Cairo)
Musée du Louvre (Paris): 5, 78, 80, 82
Musée Royal des Beaux-Arts (Antwerp): 82
Museo Archeologico (Florence): 76, 104
Museo Archeologico (Naples): 104
Museo Ginori see Museo Richard-Ginori della Manifattura di Doccia
Museo Internazionale e Biblioteca della Musica (Bologna): 113
Museo Richard-Ginori della Manifattura di Doccia (Sesto Fiorentino): X, 94, 104
Museum of Fine Arts (Boston): 78

Nakht: 61
Naples: 61, 104, 106
    Museo Archeologico: 104
    Villa della Favorita: 106
Napoleon Bonaparte (1769-1821): X, 5, 6, 45, 76, 94
Napolitano, Giorgio: IX
Nassibian, H. (active 20th century): 64
National Museum of Egyptian Civilization (Cairo, Fustat area): 29
Naucratis: 17
Nebo (cigarettes): 136
Neferet (wife of Senuseret II): 10
Nefertiti: 134, 136
Negri, Antonello: X, 117, 119
New York: 94, 104, 124, 131, 134, 136
    Cooper-Hewitt Museum: 94, 104
    Metropolitan Museum of Art: 131
New Zealand Tablet: 106
Nil see Nile
Nile: X, 13, 14, 21, 45, 46, 50, 62, 75, 132, 134
Nile Hilton Hotel (Cairo): 23
Nile Navigation Company: 10
Nilo see Nile
Nincheri, Leopoldo (active second half 19th century): 94
Nofretete see Nefertiti
Nubia: 46, 54, 68
Nubie see Nubia

Obelisk of Senuseret I (Heliopolis): 50
Octavian Augustus (63 BC - AD 14): 12
Ombos Cigarette Company Cairo Egypt: 136
Opéra (Paris): X, 87, 92
Opera House (Cairo): 104
Oriental Institute (Chicago): 62
Orsel, Victor (1795-1850): 78
O'San (cigarettes): 82, 132, 134
Osiris: 124, 134

Palagi, Pelagio (1775-1860): 106
Palais de Gizeh see Giza Palace under Giza
Palestine: 50, 68, 64
Palazzo Bonora (Bologna): 87
Palazzo Dal Monte (Bologna): 87
Palazzo del Quirinale (Rome): 92
Palazzo di Città (Turin): 92
Palazzo Reale (Turin): 92
Palazzo Rossi (Bologna): 87
Palazzo Sanguinetti (Bologna): 106, 113
Palazzo Vacchi (Imola): 92
Pallottino, Paola: 124

Palmolive: 132
Paoletti, Pietro (1801-1847): 76, 78
Paris: 17, 45, 46, 50, 68, 75, 76, 80, 87, 92, 131
    Académie des Inscriptions et Belles-Lettres: 46
    Académie des Sciences: 45
    Collège de France: 68
    Institut de France: 29
    Musée du Louvre: 5, 78, 80, 82
    Opéra: X, 87, 92
    Opera House see Opéra
    Universal Exhibition: 46, 50, 54, 61
Parliament (Cairo): 26
Pashed: X
Pasquino: 120, 122
Percy, Algernon George (1810-1899): 6
Peridis (active last decades 19th century): 54
Peridis & Co. (active last decades 19th century): 54
Peridis & Georgiladakis (active last decades 19th century): 54
Pesci, Andrea (active middle 19th century): 87
Philae: 70, 75, 82
Photoglob: 64
Piacentini, Patrizia: IX, 3, 5, 43, 45, 85, 87, 129, 131
Piccadilly (London): 45
Pimpa, Leo Cina: 124
Pinacoteca di Brera (Milan): 76
Pius IX (1792-1878): 87
P. Lorillard Tobacco Co.: 136
Poggio a Caiano: 92
    Villa Reale Medicea: 92
Pompei, Mario (1903-1958): 122, 124
Pompey's Column (Alexandria): 50
Pont-Beyrouth: 136
Port Said: 54, 61, 132, 134, 136
Poulides Bros. (cigarettes): 134
Poussin, Nicolas (1594-1665): 124
Poynter, Edward-John (1836-1919): 78
Prisse d'Avennes, Achilles Constant Théodore Émile (1807-1879): 80
Psamtek: 134
Punch: 120

Qasr Ibrim: 46
Quibell, James Edward (1867-1935): 28, 29, 64
    Quibell Collection: 29
Qurnet Murai: 134
    Tomb of Amenhotep Huy (TT 40): 134

Raccolte Musei Fratelli Alinari (Florence): 87
Rameses II see Ramesses II
Ramesses II: 14, 21
Ramsès II see Ramesses II
Real Accademia Centrale (Bologna): 92
Reale Casino del Gombo (San Rossore): 92
Record Papier Pour Cigarettes: 134
Reed, Edward Tennyson (1860-1933): 120
Reisner, George Andrew (1867-1942): 29
Re Piramidone: 127
Rhoné, Arthur (1836-1910): 13
Richard (factory): 113
Richard, Giulio (1812-1886): 113
Richard-Ginori (factory): 113
Richard-Ginori Museum see Museo Richard-Ginori della Manifattura di Doccia
Rijksmuseum (Amsterdam): 80
Roberts, David (1796-1864): 45, 78
Robichon, Clément (1906-1999): 64, 68
Robida, Albert (1848-1926): 122
Rockfeller, John D. (1839-1937): 28
Rockefeller, Mauzé Abigail "Abby" "Babs" (1903-1976): 28
Rockfeller Milton Simpson, Marilyn Ellen (1931-1980): 28
Rome: 75, 78, 80, 82, 92, 131
    Accademia di Francia: 78
    Galleria Nazionale d'Arte Moderna: 75
    Palazzo del Quirinale (Salone dei Corazzieri): 92
Rosellini, Gaetano (1796-1863): 76
Rosellini, Ippolito (1800-1843): 45, 76

Royal Air Force: 68, 70
Royal Archives (Windsor): 106
Royal Collection (London): 106

S. Anargyros: 136
Saint Clement (internment camp, Malta): 68
Saïs: 17
Sala delle Signore (Bologna, Caffè del Corso): 87
Sala di Vendita *see* Sale Room
Sale Room (Cairo Egyptian Museum): 26, 28, 29
Sale Room (Giza Museum): 28, 29
Saletta Egizia (Bologna, Palazzo Sanguinetti): 106,
        113
Salgari, Emilio Carlo Giuseppe Maria (1862-1911):
        124
Salone dei Corazzieri (Rome, Palazzo del
        Quirinale): 92
Salonique: 136
Samsoun: 136
San Giovanni in Persiceto: 87
Sanguinetti, Angelo (1818-1888): 106
San Rossore: 92
        Reale Casino del Gombo: 92
Saqqara: 17, 29, 122, 132, 134
        Serapeum: 6, 13
        Tomb of Psamtek: 134
Saqqarah *see* Saqqara
Sassetti, Luigi (active 19th century): 46
Saüberli's Cigarettes: 134
Saulcy, Félicien de (1807-1880): 10, 12
Savoia (family): 92
Sayedah Zeinab area (Cairo): 6
Schroeder-Cie Zurich: 64
Sebah, Jean-Pascal (1872-1947): 5, 21, 23, 50,
        54, 87
Sebah, Pascal (1823-1886): 54
Sehel: 70
Seif, Georges (?-1942): 64
Sem Bini (active first decades 20th century): 113
Senuseret I (12th Dynasty): 50
Senuseret II (12th Dynasty): 10
Serapeum (Saqqara): 6, 13
Sergio Reggi '900 Collection (APICE): 122, 124
Sesto Fiorentino: X, 94
        Museo Richard-Ginori della Manifattura di
        Doccia: X, 94
Sety I (19th Dynasty): 46
Sèvres: 94
Sfinge *see* Sphinx
Sha'ban, Mohamed (19th century): 17
Shakespeare, William (1564-1616): 82
Shangai: 136
Sheikh Awad (ca. 1770-ca. 1860): 76
Sheikh 'Abd el-Qurna: 61
        Tomb of Nakht (TT 52): 61
Shepheard's Hotel (Cairo): 6, 26, 50, 61, 132, 134
Simpson, William Kelly: 28
Sironi, Marta: X, 117, 119
Smoking Specialty Store: 136
Smyrna: 136
Society for the Preservation of the Monuments
        of Ancient Egypt: 20
Solmi, Valentino (1810-1866): 87
South Africa: 132
Sphinx (Giza): 10, 14, 132
Staal, Pierre Gustave Eugene (1817-1882): 122, 124
Stanza Ottagonale (Florence, Banca d'Italia): 92
Sto – pseudonym for Sergio Tofano: 124
Strabo (58 BC-21/25 BC): 78
Stradella: 122
Suez Canal: 54, 104, 120, 122, 131
Suzanne Mubarak Library (Luxor): 61
Syria: 24, 46, 64, 68
Syrie *see* Syria

Tadious (19th century): 17
Tahrir Square (Cairo): IX, 20, 23, 24
Talbot, William Fox (1800-1877): 46
Tanis: 10, 17
Tantah: 17
Tarenghi, Enrico (1848-1938): 50

Teatro Brunetti (Bologna) *see* Theather Eleonora
        Duse (Bologna)
Teja, Casimiro (1830-1897): 120, 122
Temple d'Armachis (Giza): 6, 10
Temple of Esna: 54, 132
Temple of Kom Ombo: 46
Temple of Luxor: 62, 68
Temple of Sety I (Abydos): 46
Teynard, Félix (1817-1892): 46
Theater Eleonora Duse, former Teatro Brunetti
        (Bologna): 87
Theben *see* Thebes
Thebes: 76, 136
        West Bank: 68, 70
The Orient Cigarette Co.: 136
Thotmès III *see* Thutmose III
Thun, Mattheo: 94
Thutmose III (18th Dynasty): 23
Toddi, E.: 124
Tofano, Sergio (1886-1973): 124
Tomb of Amenhotep Huy (Qurnet Murai, TT 40):
        134
Tomb of Nakht (Sheikh 'Abd el-Qurna, TT 52): 61
Tomb of Pashed (Deir el-Medina, TT 3): X
Tomb of Psamtek (Saqqara): 134
Torelli, Jafet (active second half 19th century): 94
Toussoun, Mohamed Pasha (1853-1876): 61
Tunisia: 64
Turin: 92, 94, 120
        Egyptian Museum: 120
        Palazzo di Città: 92
        Palazzo Reale: 92
Turkey: 132
Tutankhamun (18th Dynasty): 131, 132

United States of America: 24, 92, 132
Universal Exhibition (London): 82
Universal Exhibition (Paris): 46, 50, 54, 61

Valley of the Kings: 23, 50
Valley Temple (of Chephren, Giza): 6, 10
Van Cleef & Arpels: 131
Vannini (assistant of Jafet Torelli, 19th century): 94
Varille, Alexandre (1909-1951): 62, 64, 68, 70
        Varille Collection: 5, 10, 24, 26, 29 , 46, 50,
        62, 64, 68
Vassalli, Luigi (1855-1899): 14, 92, 94, 104
Verdi, Giuseppe (1813-1901): 104
Vernet, Horace (1789-1863): 45
Victoria, Queen (1819-1901): 50
Vienna: 6, 50, 82
        Kunsthistorisches Museum: 6
Villa della Favorita (Naples): 106
Villa Reale Medicea (Poggio a Caiano): 92
Villani, Filippo (1813-?): 76

West Bank (Thebes): 68, 70
Wilkinson, (Sir) John Gardner (1797-1875): 5, 80
Windsor: 106
        Royal Archives: 106
Winter Palace (Luxor): 64
Worthington, George Vigers (1870-1942): 68

Xanthis: 136

Yusuf Diya Effendi: 6

Zaffrani, Francesco (1847-?): 26
Zangaki, Constantin (active 1880-1915): X, 54, 61
Zangaki, Georges (active 1860-1880): X, 54, 61